A LITTLE LESS MUD

More Reminiscences of a Yorkshire Farmwife

by
Irene Megginson

Olive —

All Good Wishes

Irene Megginson

HUTTON PRESS
1989

Front cover: "Cot Nab" farm on the Yorkshire Wolds.

Published by the Hutton Press Ltd.
130 Canada Drive, Cherry Burton, Beverley
East Yorkshire HU17 7SB

Reprinted 1994

Printed and Bound by

*Clifford Ward & Co. (Bridlington) Ltd.
55 West Street, Bridlington, East Yorkshire
YO15 3DZ*

ISBN 0 907033 82 2

DEDICATION

For Jack
who has helped by checking
on what I have written, and agreed that
it is all true.

FOREWORD

The greatest reward from writing my "Dalesman" articles, and from my first book "Mud On My Doorstep", has been the response from those who have bothered to get in contact to say how interested they have been in what I have written.

Both Jack and I have had enormous pleasure from letters written by those who have led similar lives or old friends with whom we had lost touch.

Many have asked when I would continue my story — so for them I offer this account of a farmwife on the Wolds and hope they will not be disappointed in this simple story of every day happenings at *Cot Nab*.

Irene Megginson
Bishop Wilton
March 1989

Irene baking, helped by Sarah.

CHAPTER 1

The great removal took place in 1956. Jack and I, with our family of four school-children, had few regrets at leaving our home near Bridlington to move to a larger acreage, three-hundred-and-sixty, on the highest part of the Wolds, with a well-built house and good buildings on the Garrowby estate. The land was once considered very poor and in previous times we had passed those fields on our way to cattle sales in York and thought 'how remote, and what a backward countryside!'

We had even seen snow-covered corn stooks, and once I caught sight of children walking over the fields beside Garrowby Hill, obviously returning from school, and thought how hard life must be on this particular area of the Wolds.

However, by 1956, the use of improved fertilisers, and farming methods in general, had increased output and Jack was just happy to have the challenge of this new life under a good landlord. After all, his family had farmed Wold land since the 1770's and he had been reluctant to leave the Duggleby farm in the 1930's. Now, at Cot Nab, with its somewhat absurd name, he felt more at home on the chalky hills.

The house was foursquare, and solidly built by the Sykes of Sledmere in 1878 and sold to the Halifax family in 1917. The rooms were lofty with high sash windows, and the house seemed flooded with light after our low, damp and rather dark house near the coast.

The previous tenant had partitioned off one end of this large house to make a workman's cottage with three bedrooms. We also had only three bedrooms, though spacious, so we bought a bed settee for the dining room to accommodate the visitors we enjoyed entertaining. Extra children could sleep in the girls' room and there was space on the large landing to put a camp bed behind a screen. We took our man Henry with us, newly married now, and they too settled in well.

My chief joy was mains electricity and two flush toilets. The house was cold, but we were used to that, and could have extra warm areas around the Yorkist range in the kitchen, or by the dining and sitting room fires where Jack delighted in building up a great blaze for us all to huddle round. The windows had folding wooden shutters which helped to keep out the draughts as our curtains were unlined cretonne.

The electric cooker was simply wonderful. We took it over, as it belonged to the Electricity Board, and it had a grill, decent sized oven and two rings with a square plate, too. Heavenly! AND there was an electric washing machine with a powered wringer.

The Yorkist range, unlike the one I had cooked on for fourteen years, wasn't as good, or perhaps I had lost the patience to deal with it, so this was used mostly for its back-boiler and the oven for drying kindling or warming plates.

There was a large airing cupboard around the hot water cylinder, and in a similar cupboard on the other side of the fireplace a deep white sink had been installed behind folding doors. I never really liked that arrangement, though it looked tidy when shut away.

We took the heavy old wooden airing rack made by Uncle J.O., and he arrived to fix it on its pulleys. On the day we moved, he also brought a young sycamore tree in his old car and planted it in a corner of the garden near the front gate. Now it is a mature tree and is a memorial to that kind, hard-working man, who visited us regularly till he died aged eighty.

The children were thrilled with the size of the house, and being so near the main road to Bridlington, friends could come by bus for the day. I remember a lively game of "The Grand Old Duke of York" on the landing one wet day soon after we moved in.

There was some decorating to tackle, and mother-in-law would come and stay to help with that. I covered all the hall and landing woodwork with the wonderful new "one coat" Luxol in pale grey and it lasted for many years. With ten doors and wide mouldings, plus deep skirting boards, it was no wonder I was glad to cut out undercoats of paint!

With so many things needed on the farm, money was scarce for household goods, so there was still much make-do-and-mend. We had mostly new curtains, as the old ones wouldn't fit the high windows, and were glad the former tenants had left those in both rooms.

We had a new carpet for the dining room with stained surrounds, but took over the nearly new Wilton stair and landing carpets which, in pale green, seemed very luxurious. They are still in use, though beginning to show signs of wear!

The kitchen — devoid of "units" of course — had our large old table with new lino tacked on the top, and the painted dresser from my childhood home now had a stainless steel top with a pan shelf underneath. The huge old wardrobe again changed its image. Originally built for a wealthy child in the 1880's to hold her clothes, toys and hats — yes, there was a specially deep drawer to hold them — it had been grained to look like satin walnut.

My mother bought it from a neighbour, the original hat-wearing child, when I was young. It looked somehow castle-like in appearance with hanging cupboards on either side of double doors above a big chest of drawers and was surmounted by turret-like embellishments. It was an imposing piece of furniture and luckily took to pieces for the removal.

At Kingsfield it had still held childrens' clothes in the kitchen, the driest place in the house! Before we left, a joiner put shelves in both cupboards and I painstakingly repainted it in cream, with red panels. It looked very smart in our new kitchen, housing all the things one now puts in units, and very much easier to reach. Two of the long drawers in the chest were divided so the children could have a section each for their special use. Groceries, china, glass, and various other things, were all stowed away. Before moving I had painted all cake and storage tins in green and red labelling them with a fine brush. There were no fancy pottery jars to put on display in those days.

The floor was brick, the oblong kind, so we put down an oldish patterned carpet with clipped rugs on top, and I did the brick surrounds with cardinal polish.

Of course we had a vast dairy and storeroom-cum-office, and there was much walking to and fro between them and the kitchen. In the early days there were still the wooden gantrys in the storeroom which had originally been the milk dairy. Bowls of cream would have been fixed in place on the gantrys and at one end of the room a square concrete base showed where the separator had been fixed.

We all loved the beautiful countryside around us, and I never tired of the views from the kitchen windows with the wood, mostly larch, to one side of the deep-sided dale, the arable fields on the other side, and in the foreground the paddock where cattle, sheep or ponies grazed according to the season. The paddock had Roman entrenchments, the remains of a chalk pit, and dew pond, with a flat area which was later much used for schooling horses.

7

There was a gravel drive and a lawn in front of the house. The front door was seldom used, though at one time there must have been a pathway from the hand gate near the roadside.

The farm buildings around a large foldyard were, like the house, solid and well built. There was a good cowhouse, where our new Ayrshires were installed, a cooler house, calf boxes, pig places, and a stable which was handy for the house.

Wagon sheds housed tractors and implements and there was a Dutch barn in the stackyard with buildings away from the house, and a concrete pathway. The mud, as at Kingsfield, had receded, thus a little less mud appeared on my doorstep!

CHAPTER 2

We were all delighted with our village which was less than two miles away down a narrow lane between tree-lined banks which reminded me of Devon days. The village is six-hundred feet below the highest field of the farm, so the lane was steep, as our children soon discovered when walking to the village school. Not so bad running down in the morning, but a long way when puffing up in the afternoon.

There was a very good headmaster, Mr. Owens, and the children soon adapted to the change from the larger school in Bridlington. Tony and Jennifer only stayed one term though. Our good new neighbour, John Stringer, had a son the same age as Tony who also needed a change of school, and they were allowed to go to Market Weighton where a new secondary modern school had been built.

Their daily journeys were quite a marathon effort as the boys cycled down the six miles to Pocklington station where they caught a train, and repeated the performance at night, with a lot of pushing uphill. What a joy when they reached the moped age!

Jennifer soon heard she had passed the eleven plus exam, so had reluctantly to become a boarder at Bridlington High School, as travelling to York daily would have meant a seven-thirty start from the village. Jack was too busy at that time of morning to be tied to taking her down on a regular basis.

We soon became involved in village life with the church, W.I. and school activities. There were various fund raising efforts, particularly for the new playing fields, the land for which Lord Halifax had recently given to the village. There was a shop and a post office, but we were well served with vans for meat, fish, groceries and even a travelling chemist.

The main grocery order was taken fortnightly, as at our other farm, with the traveller coming up from Pocklington and the order being carried in the next day to be unpacked on the dairy shelf.

We had a large grass field, apart from the rest of our land, which was situated at the foot of the steep lane, and known as Wilton grass. This was sheer delight to myself and the children. A flat area with large trees at one side of the old moat, long since dry, which once

"Our village", Bishop Wilton.

surrounded the Archbishop's Palace in the Middle Ages. The field was divided from the hillier parts by a narrow winding stream crossed by either a fallen tree trunk in wet weather, or jumped over at the shallow side where one often landed with a foot in the mud.

The hillsides above a line of trees had numerous bramble bushes and in spring a mass of primroses and violets grew under their shade while more flourished on the higher slopes under a wooded area with elm, beeches and field maples. Standing up there on clear days, the views were magnificent. Below was the red-roofed village with the tall spire of St. Edith's church, and beyond the Vale of York with patterned fields stretching to the misty hills of the Pennines. Once, a never to be forgotten sight in a late spell of cold weather, we saw the Pennines snow-capped in April sunlight.

This new countryside, while of little use for cycling activities, was wonderful for riding, and Jack and I enjoyed our spare time exploring our new environment with the three girls on horseback. We soon knew the tracks through the dales and the pretty lanes down to Kirby Underdale, Thixendale, Bishop Wilton and Givendale.

We found good, friendly, and helpful neighbours all around us, but saw more of the Stringers and Beaulahs, whose families were soon constant visitors as they got on very well with our four.

Our old friends came to see us with their children who were thrilled with the change in our surroundings, while no doubt also appreciating our "mod cons" after all the years of roughing it at Kingsfield. More local friends, and relations, often called and being nearer to most of them was a bonus, though some were further away including my Mother, Lill, and Uncle J.O., but the last frequently drove over in his old Lanchester to organise a vegetable garden for us.

Many plants were less productive on the exposed Wold land, and although the shelter belt, so necessary on all such farms, helped a lot, there were always some vegetables and garden flowers which

Irene helps to build the garden wall.

11

refused to thrive. To Uncle J.O.'s disgust we spent many hours extending the lawn to make a tennis court as we, and our family, were keen on the game. We had also been given a net and marking wheel to encourage us.

Jack built low walls of old brick with steps down to the lower lawn where we could sit (if there was time) away from the main road traffic. We made a raised flower bed in front of the garage and planted rose trees. "Well, Irene," said Uncle J.O., "I'd have thought a few cabbages would have been more useful!"

CHAPTER 3

Jack was finding many changes with the running of a Wold farm. One was growing seed potatoes and there was much to learn in that department.

Luckily, our neighbours John Stringer and Arthur Beaulah had been in on this comparatively new venture since the idea was first conceived. Bruce Megginson and Charley Foster had also experimented with this idea, helped by Mr. Fearnside from the Ministry.

The High Wold Seed Potato Growers Association was formed, and Jack became a member with the art of "roqueing" to learn for one thing. This involved the pulling out of diseased plants from the crop before inspection by officers of the Board, in order to obtain the necessary certificate. If "A"s were awarded, we were very pleased. Labels were issued for "Certified Wold Seed". Meetings were held, often in Huggate pub, and Jack met up with other potato growers. Later, a shield was donated to be won each year, and once we were proud to display it on the hall sideboard.

Much time was spent in hoeing spuds in pre-spray days and there were mangolds ("wuzzles" in our language), kale and turnips. Oats and wheat were grown in our early years, but the bulk of the corn we grew was barley. In the first harvests we still used a binder as well as the new combine, a Massey-Harris 726, which had been a generous moving present from Mother and cost £500.

I was called out to help to "pick" on the stack, but most of the corn was combined and was taken to Medforths in Bridlington to be dried. Later, the Stringers installed a continuous drier and we took grain there, while the sheaves from the old way of harvest were put through the hammer mill.

After a specially bad harvest, the last of the sheaves were so rotten they were dumped in a pit, and that was the end of an era. Never again did we see fields of stooked corn. The combine was now the harvest king.

Shepherding was often difficult with the vast rough pasture in the dale, but net setting on turnips continued, and was hard work too. Lambing time meant non-stop, round the clock, attention to ewes and lambs. Jack often sat up at night in the kitchen, missing the old couch which had now been put in a shed. Years later I regretted letting it go to ruin as *chaise longue* were in great demand!

The three girls, when at home, loved to help at lambing time. I sometimes felt annoyed when washing up was waiting and they all pushed back chairs from the table to rush out after Daddy. I eventually put my foot down and insisted that at least one stayed to help me, but it wasn't a popular idea.

I still did big bakings, appreciating the electric oven, but there was plenty to do, and I was glad of some help in the house from whoever lived in the cottage. There were several changes of families there over the years, and after Henry, with wife and little son, decided to go back to a job near his old home, the Ayrshires were sold, but we still reared calves.

Chickens were reared for Thornbers, with much washing and packing of eggs, usually an evening job. The chickens were very stupid about learning to perch so we had to keep a careful watch on the silly birds at one stage of their lives, to prevent them huddling in a heap which was likely to smother some of them.

One washday, when the drying ground was out in the paddock (later moved to the garden), the calves had fun and games with the newly washed clothes. Too late I rushed out to shoo them off. Some garments were beyond repair. However, being a thrifty soul, I did the best I could to save them, although shirts, pyjamas, my nightie, and some blouses suddenly became the short sleeved variety!

This was an era of farm walks and discussion societies. Firms organised demonstrations and there were visits to experimental farms. Locally there was the Bishop Wilton Show and Jack was soon on the committee. Later he was elected Treasurer, but didn't care for this job so cleverly invited our friends, the Smiths from Kent, for the weekend of the Show! Wilf was an accountant, and he virtually took over on Show day, with figures all totted up by midnight, often bringing work back to our dining room table.

As August Bank Holiday approached each year, the first weekend in August, we thought up fancy dresses for the girls and friends to wear for this class on ponies. There was always a last minute panic to get the costumes finished, plus rushing round cleaning tack and riding clothes for other classes. With weekend guests, picnics to pack and sometimes entries for the W.I. tent to take down, the day started early and finished late with everyone pretty well exhausted.

The Show in those days was THE day of the year for entertaining

Tony in the train room.

with almost every family in the village attending, many walking to the field and back with the meeting up of friends seldom seen, as few villagers owned cars.

When the next people came to the cottage, we had the landing partition moved back to include the doorway of another bedroom, and so acquired the convenient addition of an extra room upstairs. This was for Tony, and I redecorated it for the total sum of twenty-seven shillings and sixpence. We were extra hard up then, but it looked nice, and later I added a wall of vintage cars when such papers were fashionable.

The small inlaid mahogany bedroom suite was bought in a sale-room for ten pounds. I sent the marble topped washstand to have the doors made into a fireside stool, but this was never successful. Today, the washstand would be worth a "bomb".

Tony was very mechanically minded, having little interest in school other than technical drawing classes and agricultural science. He was a great help on the farm, always busy, and never bored. He would spend hours with his model railway, set up in the store room, or in concocting some elaborate invention. The bedroom became a mass of wires, all attached to something, so cleaning days were a nightmare.

We had a small cottage in the village for a farm worker, and the tractor driver lived there. Another chap cycled up the hill, or rather pushed part of the way, and on the return journey at night went down in two minutes at literally break neck speed.

Although hard at work for most of the day, Jack found time on light evenings and at weekends to ride with me or the girls. He also took us to see our respective mothers in Bridlington, as I had never learned to drive a car. In some ways — people who could drive pointed this out — we got out together as a family, whereas a farm wife who drives is often told, "You go with the children, I'm too busy!"

My neighbour, Hetty Beaulah, loved to drive and often took me to York or with the children to the swimming baths, to various meetings, social occasions, and sometimes, to Challis's for garden plants. That was in the early days of plant nurseries when no one could have visualised the growth into massive garden centres, selling almost everything.

CHAPTER 4

On July 1st 1956, in our first summer, we attended the little ceremony on the roadside near Garrowby Hill top, when the Archbishop of York dedicated the crucifix recently erected by the First Earl of Halifax to the memory of King George VI.

The first Earl and his Countess were truly wonderful people. They visited us personally soon after we moved in to welcome us to the estate. On another occasion we were honoured to be asked to lend my old cob Flicka for a few days, for one of his Lordship's elderly friends who was visiting, to ride round the countryside. So, off went Flicka for a few days' residence in the Hall Stables! She couldn't tell us whether she had enjoyed herself, but we had a personal visit from his Lordship to thank us for the loan of such a "charming" pony.

It was still the custom in the 'fifties for the landlord to ask for the use of a room in a suitable farmhouse in which shooting parties could eat their lunch. I had nothing to do when we received such a request, other than to light the dining room fire. Food was brought in by the butler-cum-handyman, and the front door came into use, so this "intrusion" bothered us very little. Afterwards, Lord Halifax came through to the kitchen to thank us, and I always regretted not asking him to sign his autobiography, "Fullness of Days" which I had recently bought and read with great interest.

In 1958, we had the pleasure, with many other tenants, of attending the Golden Wedding celebrations at Garrowby. This was a memorable occasion held in an enormous marquee erected on one of the few flat areas of the parkland around the Hall. Tenants and estate workers were personally greeted before having a lovely meal followed by speeches, toasts and a firework display.

The wedding of Lord Halifax's grand-daughter, Susan Wood, with Brigadier Ian Watson, took place in York Minster in 1959 and again all tenants were invited. This was a very happy occasion for us all, with a reception in the Assembly Rooms. On the return journey I think some car drivers would have been considerably over the limit, had there been such things as breath tests, after enjoying rather too much champagne!

It was with great sadness that we attended a simple funeral service in the beautiful but tiny church in Kirby Underdale when the beloved "Old Lord" died as the year also reached its end. This modest man, in typical fashion, chose his resting place behind the church where he loved to worship. Under an ancient Spanish chestnut tree, his grave faces the beautiful hills and fields of countryside where he knew not only all the occupants of farms and cottages, but every stick and stone as well.

CHAPTER 5

With three pony-mad daughters, we were soon very much involved in the Middleton Hunt and the Pony Club. Much of our spare time was taken up by meetings of various kinds, and during the winter months we followed hounds ourselves with the girls joining us in school holidays, or going off on their own with someone to keep an eye on them.

Jack seldom had time to go during the week, but I took the odd day off. It was hard work to get things done the night before, with tack cleaning, and cooking ahead, then an early start on the morning to get my pony groomed and myself dressed in readiness for the hack to the meet which was sometimes as far as fifteen miles away.

One had to be keen, and it wasn't because I was a good rider either. Flicka "battled along" the roads at a fast, bumpy trot, and the miles were covered in good time. I went because of my love of horses, the sight of hounds working, and the beauty of the countryside in all weathers. There was the excitement of wondering whether I could keep up, avoid jumps, and pull up in time to avoid crashing into a gatepost, as Flicka had a hard mouth so her braking power wasn't too good!

I am not trying to justify the questionable ethics of fox hunting, but I must say I have never met a "blood thirsty" follower, or seen a fox torn to pieces alive with huntsmen doing a sort of tribal dance, as some "antis" would have it. The whoops when a fox is killed is to encourage the hounds. After the first one's teeth meet the neck of the fox, death is instant.

Most hunting people have a strange sympathy with the fox. They admire his cunning, and are usually thankful if Charlie saves his brush for another day, while realising that the fox population must be kept down. Ask any sheep farmer, or poultry keeper, what cruelties these vicious creatures inflict.

I often had a young neighbour who rode with me to the meets, and one particular day we left the village in bright sunshine to ride to Sutton-on-Derwent. When we reached this village the sun had disappeared and we were blanketted in fog. After standing around for some time at the meet, hoping the weather would clear, the

Master decided to return to Givendale where he knew the sun was shining.

Most people got a lift in horseboxes, and the car followers were all right, but Pat and I, plus a few others, had to retrace our tracks by riding all the way back again! We must have ridden more than twenty miles before we joined in a good run in beautiful country with blue skies above us. At least I was near home when we decided to call it a day. Sometimes, when riding along the Givendale road after a long hack home with aching legs, the sight of Cot Nab chimneys on the hilltop was as welcome as an oasis to the desert traveller.

During the week there were seldom many followers, and people were so friendly and helpful. The majority "did" their own horses, so after a long, muddy, exhausting day, there was the feeding and rubbing down of one's horse. Tack had to be washed off too, before thinking of feeding oneself, after only a chocolate bar all day, and the hope of a luxurious soak in a hot bath. I sometimes forfeited the latter till later if the children were home from school, and everyone was waiting for a meal. But it was all wonderfully worthwhile with the memory of the day to mull over as the pain of aching limbs receded.

Jack and Tony in 1958 with the new Land-Rover, and snow too!

The girls were very good doing their share of stable work and we wouldn't have let them have ponies if it had been otherwise, but how I often cursed the muddy garments. Newly washed bridles and saddles often decorated the kitchen. One morning, I went down early, rushing as usual. I jumped up on a chair to pull down girths from the airer, and on jumping down put my foot in a bowl of water left underneath to catch the drips. I don't remember what I said!

Pony Club rallies were greatly enjoyed. Sometimes we only had to go as far as the outskirts of our village where an enthusiastic mother, Mrs Hague, organised activity meetings in the summer and film shows or quizzes in the winter. We had a Landrover by then, but no car, so could take two ponies in the trailer if rallies were further away. Hunter trials were fun too, often joining up with our friends, the Mason family, with more children and ponies than we had!

The summer camps organised by the Pony Club meant a great deal of preparation with all threee girls and ponies to be catered for. I shudder now to think of all the packing up beforehand, to say nothing of the unpacking when the week was over, with mountains of dirty washing.

With lists to be gone through in triplicate, it was no joke. Apart from pony equipment, and children's clothing, camp beds were needed with bedding, as well. We hadn't a supply of sleeping bags in those early days and I remember making bags from flannelette sheets. Pieces of carpet were useful for bedside rugs, as well as groundsheets, for grass could be cold first thing in the morning.

Our first camp, though, was held at Brandsby Hall, where the youngsters slept dry and cosy in the old squash court. All these camps over the years were mostly held in the grounds of stately homes. Mums were expected to give a day's help in the kitchens, and it took a lot of organisation by the committee to feed as many as sixty children and adults. Jack's job was to help in putting up the tents, all army types, and then taking them down at the end of camp.

The equipment was often primitive, and disused servants quarters in the old halls were not the most convenient places in which to cook and serve meals, but we all managed to improvise.

As I peeled or cleaned endless vegetables while standing beside a row of Victorian sinks, I thought of the servants who had slaved away in those vast semi-basement rooms with only roofs and tree-tops to look out on. I don't expect they had much time to gaze out of the high windows, but they would be well fed and comfortably housed with the comradeship of fellow workers. Thus, they were better off than many folk in those days.

The warren of small rooms opening off the main kitchen and servants hall was a revelation. All stone flagged, there was a game larder, housekeeper's room, butler's pantry, many store rooms and an ice house. The latter was built into thick stone walls with a tunnel-like entrance There would have been such a large number of staff, too. My Mother-in-law lived near this particular Hall in her youth and recalled how half the staff attended morning service in the nearby church, and the other half went to Evensong.

CHAPTER 6

We soon got used to snow. In fact, there was a covering over the fields as if to greet us on our first awakening in our new home. Most winters saw us snowed up at some stage, but only the worst and prolonged spells remain in my memory.

One of these brought us an exhausting experience on New Year's Eve in 1958. Jack drove the old Humber Supersnipe to a twenty-first party in Filey. There was no sign of snow on the way there, but as we left in the early hours of the first day of January flakes of snow appeared on the windscreen. Jack decided not to risk the Wold roads and for safer travelling chose the Malton route.

The snow increased in volume, but we had no trouble till we reached Birdsall. Here we stuck on a hill, but we managed to get going again. That old car was the worst type for slippery surfaces and finally we ground to a halt on the next hill after passing through the village.

Tony keeping warm in an ex Air-Force coat.

I could only think of bedding down in the car till help came, but Jack was made of sterner stuff, and was also worried about Tony and the girls at home. He had an overcoat over his dinner jacket suit, but only patent leather shoes. I had luckily taken fur lined boots to travel in, but had only a waist length fur cape over my fashionable ballet-style evening dress! So I wrapped myself Indian-wise in the car rug, and off we went!

The snow was only ankle deep and little more fell during the night as we plodded on and on, trudging up hills slowly and stopping occasionally to get our breath back. We passed darkened, quiet farms, where I imagined the occupants snug in their beds. I even envied the hens cosy perches above straw as we passed a lighted deep litter house.

My right leg had been aching for some time as we thankfully reached our back door at six o'clock! We had walked about eight miles after leaving the car. The family were all asleep so no one had worried about us! I filled a hot water bottle and blissfully curled up in bed, while Jack had a bath and changed into his working clothes. Fortified by cups of tea, he went out to see to the stock, but later in the day had a good sleep in his fireside chair. Incidentally, his shoes survived well!

There was more snow during that day, and Arthur Beaulah took his Landrover to help Jack rescue the car. I limped round the house after a late start, preparing a meal of roast goose for guests previously invited, but only two of them, Elizabeth and Leonard, braved the bad travelling conditions to join us.

In February of that year, our annual Hunt Ball took place in Pocklington. This was always a great social occasion with a good crowd there, and it made a handsome profit in spite of the tickets costing twelve shillings and sixpence.

Lord and Lady Irwin ran our local committee which mostly consisted of farmers and their wives. All refreshments were home made, and this meant much hard work and preparation, but we all worked well together to feed a few hundred guests. The worst part was loading up the car with all the trays of food, dishes and bowls plus jugs of soup, the last served "on departure".

That afternoon there was a little snow, but not enough to really worry us as we prepared the refreshments at Oak House in Pocklington. We usually had a few friends in for drinks before setting off to the dance, taking with us Mrs Wilson from the cottage who, with a few more helpers, did all the washing up.

All went well as usual, ending with a "Post Horn Gallop" and "Auld Lang Syne", and after collecting all our bits and pieces, we set off for home about two-thirty. As we approached the hill up to Givendale, we realised there was no hope of reaching home by car. Arthur Beaulah offered to come back our way in his "Austin Gypsy", after taking someone to the village, but he too got stuck and had to return by another route.

We, with a few other committee cars, came to a halt near Givendale church, and some went into Cecil Jackson's house for shelter. Jack and I, plus Mrs Wilson, set off to walk the mile and half to Cot Nab, but the snow was deep, and before we had covered much ground, Mrs Wilson became distressed in her breathing. Jack told me to take her back to the Jacksons while he went on, with some difficulty, across country where part of the fields were clear as the wind had swirled the snow into the lane.

Mrs Wilson and I were welcomed in the warm house, given hot drinks, and armchairs to rest in, as all beds and sofas were already occupied! We slept fitfully and were rescued the next morning when Jack reached Givendale on a tractor. Later, with Tony to help they got the car home too, and we thankfully had an afternoon by the fire.

CHAPTER 7

It was quite a relief to part with the old Humber which was so useless in winter conditions, and to buy our first Landrover, though for two years it was our only vehicle. We enjoyed the better views when driving around at a higher level, and the padded bench seating in the back gave room for family and friends. We thought it wonderful to be able to go for picnics on roads labelled "Unsuitable for motors".

In cold weather the bedrooms were almost freezing, although electric blankets were a new luxury. We had only recently parted with our old feather bed. There was much in the newspapers at that time about "feather bedded farmers", but I knew we were only feather bedded because we couldn't afford a "spring interior"! At last, for Christmas, I was given a beautiful gold covered "Slumberland" which my Mother, on Jack's instructions, had had delivered to her house as a surprise for me when we arrived for lunch on Christmas Day.

It was loaded into the Landrover afterwards, with children and other presents, and what a joy to me to finish for ever the daily shaking up of feathers! On cold winter mornings it often took all my courage to leave the comfortable bed to dress as quickly as possible, with many gasps as cold garments were pulled on before rushing down to the kitchen where an industrial size electric fan heater was a quick form of heating.

I disliked cleaning bedrooms when the weather was cold, and often wore gloves to do a quick dash with the Hoover. We heard tales of tenants in the old days who found the chamber pots frozen over, and I can quite believe them. No wonder the farmers used to choose bedrooms at the back of the house over the kitchen, partly to keep an ear open for any trouble with the stock in the yards, but also for warmth, I'm sure.

The front rooms downstairs probably only had a fire in the grates at weekends, if that, for they were mostly kept for "company" use, especially in the depression years. We tried to make use of both rooms during winter evenings and weekends in order to keep them aired, and so moved from one to the other.

26

We had our first good sledging experiences, too, with gatherings of friends joining us in the dale. It could be quite hair raising going at great speed while hurtling down the steeper slopes, and even the more gradual slope of the long valley could give some anxious moments. All this was a novelty after living in the flat countryside near the coast, where deep snow seldom lasted long in any case. Sometimes we joined the larger gatherings of winter sports enthusiasts in Millington Pastures. As a child in Hull, visiting the much loved Pastures, I never visualised living in such lovely countryside and taking my children there with their toboggans.

CHAPTER 8

Tatie-time was always a headache, and still is, despite modern equipment. But with primitive methods of spinning out, hand picking and the making of pies, it was an especially harassing time of the farming year.

We had gangs of pickers, sometimes with children joining in during the autumn school holiday. One old diary records, "Ten children — six shillings each", and our family were anxious to help too. However, the first few days were hard with much complaining about aching backs! Several women were brought up from the village, and a good cheerful lot they were too.

I gave "looances" both morning and afternoon and soon acquired a great selection of mugs, cups, and plastic beakers of one sort or another. In 1957, for some reason, we resorted to getting labour exchange men who came from Hull by train and had to be collected at Pocklington station each morning. An unlikely looking gang, unsuitably dressed and being quite unused to field work, I think Jack was glad when he could finish with their efforts. I expect they were glad too!

In spite of the worry of getting up taties, we usually had a good party on Bonfire Night, as we had done at Kingsfield, and everyone expected it to continue. A huge fire was built up gradually in a field a safe distance from the farm yard and we delighted in making a life-sized Guy. In fact, one year he was so realistic that we were amused to find Glen the sheepdog sitting beside him near the stable. We had propped up Mr. Fawkes before he was transported to the field. Obviously he smelled like the Boss, economically dressed in cast off working clothes.

One year I remember having an ancient armchair to put on the bonfire and with Guy sitting aloft, the whole effect was quite startling as the flames flickered around the figure before devouring the lot.

There were usually over thirty people in our kitchen after the last firework had been lit and the blaze had died down. I served hot soup from my large preserving pan and got a lasting good name in this culinary art. Actually it was just a case of some good stock plus

Colin Newlove takes "Yogi" the badger for a walk.

every sort of chopped vegetable and flavouring added. I still do this sort of soup on occasions for large parties, but now have a liquidiser and cheat by adding good packets to thicken it!

After the supper — soup was only the starter — the youngsters amused themselves and the adults adjourned to the sitting room fireside. I like to think our girls helped to wash up, but I can't remember! One year our good friend Colin Newlove, who became well-known as an animal trainer, had at that time reared a young badger called Yogi who had grown into a handsome animal unafraid of humans and with complete trust in following Colin anywhere. On this occasion her master quietly entered our sitting room with Yogi at his heels. Unsuspecting guests could scarcely believe their eyes as this beautiful creature sat up and begged for biscuits on the rug in front of the fire.

Colin not only trained badgers, even getting a pair to breed, but had great fun with various other animals with whom he had a natural affinity. He was a constant help to us with any pony problems and was himself a great character and raconteur who could reduce us to helpless laughter with his tales and his gift of mimicry. In later years he also trained an Ayrshire bull which he rode as the main ring attraction of county shows up and down the country, from the Royal Highland to the Royal Cornwall.

At home at Bugthorpe his menagerie was a great attraction whenever we had our old friends to stay with their families. "Seeing Colin" was one of their first requests on arrival. Tumbling pigeons, a tame kestrel found injured, and at one time a young deer who had also suffered injury, or a horse who could bow or "die" on request, in fact whenever you made your way to Bugthorpe, there was always some new trick to be demonstrated.

1959 was an exceptionally early harvest and in September, when all was safely gathered in, we went off in the Landrover with Colin and our girls for a glorious three days at Harewood as spectators at our first Three Day Event, little thinking of a future when, through Rachel, we were to become so involved in the horse trials world.

At that time it was all a great novelty to us, and much more relaxed than in these days. We could walk where we liked in that wonderful parkland, and, in turn, became dressage enthusiasts, cross country fanactics, and anxious supporters of our favourite horses in the final show jumping phase.

We arrived at Harewood early each morning and during the

journeys to and fro, Colin entertained us with stories in his own individual fashion. We also learned much about wildlife from this born naturalist. On our last evening, when the rest of us were ready to leave, we found Rachel lying on her stomach in front of the big scoreboard, frantically copying down the final scores of all competitors.

Before the 'fifties ended, we had a new kitchen floor of wood, due to dry rot in the cellar beams. This made life difficult as, with the kitchen out of use, I had to do cooking on the dining room hearth where I made a hob of bricks, or on the picnic stove on the dairy shelf. The front door came into constant use, and washing up was done in the little handbasin in the cloakroom.

I was very thrilled with the new inlaid linoleum floor in dark red with oblong patterns in blue, grey and yellow. It was inclined to show muddy feet or paw marks, and needed polishing too, but was an improvement on the old bricks and dusty carpet.

As the years passed, we joined in more with village life. I took part in one of the last of the W.I. concerts in the village hall, and what fun we had with rehearsals in a farm kitchen for one act dialect plays. There were other acts to make up a programme, and I'm sure the

The tennis court in use.

31

audience was appreciative, in spite of the rickety stage and rather temperamental curtains.

Once we had a great day as hosts to the Farm Women's Club, with representatives of the "Farmers Weekly" and about forty members from various parts of Yorkshire. It was a very happy occasion and an early attempt on my part at large scale catering, but the food was all of the simple farmhouse kind. The weather wasn't too kind, and few ventured to look round outside.

When the two girls came home from school they said they had never heard such a row before, with all the conversations going on and were also disgusted because in all the activity of the day I had forgotten to feed the pet lamb!

The sitting room was also improved by the purchase of blue velour curtains with fringed pelmets, the height of luxury. I ordered these in Bridlington, but Jack helped with the measurements. We were very proud when they were duly hung, but having a bill for sixty pounds was horrific. Nearly thirty years later, they are still there, redyed with pelmets discarded, but well worth that initial outlay. Unfortunately at one stage they acquired uneven stains near the hems as we had a cairn puppy who was inclined to sneak into the room to lift his leg up the precious curtains. Perhaps he was trying to express an opinion!

The stairs and landing were papered by a local husband and wife team and took thirty rolls of wallpaper. I made the mistake of choosing a pale, insignificant pattern for the well of the staircase, and it soon looked grubby. It is always rather a gamble in choosing paper, and, like most people, my choice has sometimes been rather a disaster.

On the farm, sixty-five lambs were sold for £7 each, and eight calves bought for £50. In the harvest of nineteen fifty-seven, we lost half our barley when it was beheaded by a freak hail storm. This was an unexpected setback and there was no insurance. There were no farm secretaries, and Jack slaved over the accounts with much muttering as he endeavoured to make things balance. The accountants were used to receiving cumbersome, brown paper parcels tied with string, as most farmers during that period presented the farm books in this way.

We had weathered our first years on a larger acreage and the 'sixties were upon us.

CHAPTER 9

The 'sixties were certainly "swinging" in some ways, chiefly with
the ups and downs of farming, but socially we must have had a pretty
hectic time with so many balls, dinner dances, and visits to the
theatre at York when friends often came back for a snack supper.
Occasionally we indulged in the new fashion of going out for meals,
sometimes driving quite a long way, but we were never enthusiastic
about eating out, unless for some special celebration. For me, the
company is more important than the food.

The first diary entry for 1960 reads, "Frank and Tony silage straw
etc. Frank hedging and Tony burning thorns. We took ponies to
Thorpe Hall meet. Party of us (19) went to Pony Club dance,
Brandsby Hall." In the week which followed, we visited cousins for
the evening, had Bridlington friends for the day, joined in a Pony
Club Quiz, helped to organise a Pony Club paper chase, and entertained Joan, Ken and the Beaulahs to supper.

Of course we worked hard in between, myself in the house and
Jack always doing yard work and shepherding.

After the holiday, there were the girls' trunks to pack, and the
drive back to school. All three were now away. Rachel had joined
Jennifer at Bridlington High, and Maureen, who didn't get the
eleven
plus exam, was a weekly boarder at Filey Convent. I got to the stage
of carbon-copying their weekly letters, varying pages according to
clarity, and always starting off with a personal message. Maureen
got a letter, too, of course, as post was quick and sometimes she
stayed over a weekend.

Some Bridlington pupils were amused by my system; we heard
from one of Jen's friends that she was running round one morning to
find Rachel, shouting "Can you swop? I've got two page three's".

Life was a constant round of school activities we must attend, or
exeats to prepare for. Postcards would arrive during the week,
"Please can I bring Judith, and can we have porridge pudding. I've
told her how good it is." Once Rachel added, "Sorry I can't think of
anything spicy for Postman to read!" At that time our postman, a
great character and good friend, used to sit in his car having a little
read before coming in with the mail.

A family group.

34

Not so many years before we arrived at Cot Nab, this postman had walked the long and hilly route with long distances between farms and outlying cottages. I'm not sure why he used his own car rather than an official van.

There were the usual sports days, speech days, and garden fetes which Jack usually opted out of as not being able to spare the time, and not much inclination either! I went along with the Creasers, other parents living in Pocklington, who became good friends.

Once Jack gave in to the girls' pleadings and took two ponies in the trailer. After the somewhat tedious ceremony was over, they rode on the beach and thoroughly enjoyed themselves. Having my mother, stepfather and Lill in Bridlington, and Mother-in-law in Bessingby, we could at least fit in their visits as well, thus killing several birds with one stone.

The High School boarders put on a really excellent nativity play each December in Emmanuel Church, and one year, after a short visit to friends in Manchester we were anxious to get back in time, but arrived late. We managed to slip into a pew as the performance began. "I knew you had got here," said our 'Angel' daughter. "I could see Dad's bald patch as I walked down the aisle".

They all missed farm life and often resented having to be boarders. The abolition of the eleven plus exam, and the building of a good comprehensive school in Pocklington, came just too late. Our grandchildren are happy there, and are collected by bus at the farm gate.

Tony was by now attending day release classes, and acquired some City and Guild certificates. He was much involved in the Young Farmers, and when he passed his driving test, we bought a second hand Austin Cambridge which eased the problem of his getting around to meetings and other jaunts.

For some time, Tony, with our friends of both sexes, plus our girls, had had great fun with an old Baby Austin which he had bought very cheaply. They drove this car all over the paddock, up and down the bumps, in and out of a track through the wood, all in true 'rally' fashion. The driver was often distracted by shrieks of terror, but the passengers really revelled in being scared to death. Sometimes one of the girls was behind the wheel, and the excitement increased with the many near misses while negotiating the twisting path through the trees.

We all regretted in later years letting this tough little car get

The old car in which the family had such fun.

bashed up, as it could have been a valuable asset in vintage classes.

With our comfortable little car in use, as well as the Landrover, we offered to drive my mother and stepfather to visit my older sister in Kent. We actually stayed in a small hotel, a treat for us, yet saw a lot of my sister and her friends. We also saw much of a countryside new to us, with all the orchards, hop fields and oasthouses. Tunbridge Wells is a lovely town, and we visited Rye, and other fascinating places. On our return journey, we made a detour to spend a night with old friends Margery and Ellis Bendall on their Wiltshire farm.

Whenever we go away, there always seems to be a lot I want to fit in, with people to call on, so poor Jack drives long distances in circles. He, of course, loves to visit friends too, and as long as we are not on motorways, can 'farm up' whichever county we might be passing through. In the early 'sixties, though, it was a case of going the long way round in these pre-motorway journeys.

I was still keen on giving the whole house a thorough clean each spring, often doing some painting and decorating too. Mother-in-law, before she got to the stage of being dizzy on steps, had taught me to hang paper, and while quite enjoying this job, I moaned about the height of the ceilings.

I often kept on with the 'cleaning' jobs till bed time. The kitchen walls, being gloss paint, were washed, as was the bathroom. Dairies had to be whitened, but the job was less messy with emulsion paint. It was a great relief when the bathroom and kitchen were eventually papered with 'washable' type papers, but, if the truth be known, I don't ever remember washing them!

1960 saw the last of the corn stooks, when some oat sheaves were put through the combine from the stooks, and others fed to the bullocks at the end of that rather disastrous harvest. So, "The old 'bagger' went, and two hundred and sixteen sacks were taken down to Fishers," to quote the diary. Messrs. Fishers, the agricultural firm in the village, was very handy for us and was often called out to machinery breakdowns.

Tony driving a combine in 1961.

37

The new Massey 500 was Tony's pride and joy. He looked after it with great care, so much so that when he reluctantly parted with it in 1984, it was still in remarkably good condition.

During 1960 I kept a pictorial diary for a "Farmers Weekly" competition and won £15. This seemed an enormous sum of money and people kept asking what I was going to buy, having seen illustrations of the diary in the magazine. I thought about it for a while, then, being of a practical turn of mind, bought a 'Hoover Constellation' cleaner and found it very useful.

Work, during the farming year, still consisted of much getting in of silage (we had a pit at that time), and straw, trimming bushes, burning thorns, hedging, mucking out boxes, or tarring hen huts. The field work went on as was usual with scruffing and ridging taties in pre-spray and pre-power harrow days. We bought a bale-sledge which seemed quite wonderful, but the pulling of wild oats was a tiring job, and still is, as no one has yet found a machine to do it.

Jack now clipped sheep by machine. It was a hard and sweaty job, and we were glad when the weather was good for the rather naked looking ewes to be turned out to the paddock. I was always surprised that the lambs recognised their mothers after such a transformation. There was much "maa-ing" and bleating till each family was sorted out and reunited.

Jack, Jennifer, Rachel and Maureen.

CHAPTER 10

We still appreciated the beautiful countryside which surrounded us. So many motorists rush along the York to Bridlington road thinking what a bleak place to live in, totally unaware of the pretty villages nestling under the wolds on either side.

It was a constant delight to exercise the ponies through the various dales, or round the pretty lanes to Kirby Underdale, Uncleby, Thixendale or Millington. It was good country, too, for getting horses fit as hill work hardens muscles quicker than anything.

Our friends, who came frequently, loved the car drives to Kirkham Abbey, Buttercrambe woods, and Castle Howard. My mother, in her old age, especially delighted in being driven in the Landrover round the hillside tracks in our dale, or up the steep slope of Wilton grass, which could be very bumpy.

When our children were teenagers, we tried to arrange one Landrover outing each year, with our neighbours the Stringers and

Group taken on a Land-Rover picnic with the Stringers.

family, plus one or two extra friends. The two Landrovers would be laden with passengers and food. We had several memorable days, usually choosing off the map roads, and discovering some place new to us.

The Brandsdale day stands out in memory, also one in the Bronte country. In Haworth, while looking in shop windows after 'doing' the Parsonage, we saw, liked and bought, an oak chest of drawers for £12. It was delivered to us the following day and has now increased in value and acts as our dressing table.

Another outing took place in such dreadful weather that the only way we could eat our picnic in a quarry near Hutton-le-Hole was by backing up the Landrovers and fixing a polythene sheet between to make a shelter. Later that day we discovered Kildane and Ingleby Greenhow.

We look back now at photos of these happy outings, and were delighted when the next generation also remembered them and revived the custom. Theirs was on a larger scale with extra vehicles to accommodate not only the Megginsons and Stringers, but the Rivis family, Fosters, Fullers and Meltcalfes.

With the passage of time, more up to date food was demanded by the youngsters, so baked beans, bangers and hamburgers were heated up to be eaten with the inevitable packet of crisps!

Our young teenagers didn't expect quite so much freedom, or possessions, as the grandchildren did later. There weren't so many battles over clothes, nor was it the norm to have such a large selection. Stiletto shoes were just coming into fashion with 'straight' skirts. I rather liked the frilly petticoat era, but our girls mostly wore trousers, and were not so fussy about shape, style or material. Jodhpurs still had slight flares, and were not as easy to wash. Jackets for hunting and riding were often second hand, and jockey caps with soft crowns were thought adequate. None of us wore hats when hacking!

It wasn't essential then to have the best, most up to date fashion wear, which must be a strain on the budgets of today's families.

School uniform was hated, but accepted, and the more expensive items, like High School distinctive striped blazers, and Sunday suits of green serge, could be bought second hand in school.

Tony and his friends went to ballroom dancing classes in York which were held in rooms now beautifully restored as part of Fairfax House.

We first discovered the pleasure of country dancing in those years, having first joined in with Kathy Mitchell 'calling' at a Lions Barbecue at Gara farm. We were a little apprehensive at first, but soon realised the joy of it all. I have never seen a gloomy country dancer. Later, we went regularly to dances in village halls and barns. We joined a weekly class in Pocklington, and made many good friends while enjoying the exercise. It is also excellent for the brain, as some of the dances are quite complicated to remember.

CHAPTER 11

We did some crazy things through our obsession with horses and ponies. One summer evening, Jennifer, who had now left school and was working at home before going to a farm secretarial college, Colin Newlove, Jack and I, set off for Beaulieu in the New Forest to see one of the famous pony sales. Jack was the only driver, but the roads were quiet. There was one stop for a drink and a short nap and we reached the New Forest early in the morning. It was wonderfully peaceful and fresh. We chose a pretty place to have a breakfast picnic after washing and cleaning teeth in a bubbling stream not far from the roadside.

The sale was an education to us. Never had we seen so many pony mares and foals collected up together in numerous pens. We spent an hour or two just looking round, picking out likely buys and taking in the general scene. I especially fell for two donkey mares with foals, but then, I've always loved donkeys. The trouble is, Jack can't stand them!

We were joined by Margery from Wiltshire, and much discussion went on until the 'lots' decided upon came up. Colin bought three ponies and Jack a couple of two-year-olds, a grey and a pretty chestnut with a blonde mane and tail. Transport had to be sorted out and it was decided that the cheapest way was for them to go by rail to Stamford Bridge station.

By the middle of the afternoon we were on our way, following Margery back to her farm home near Hungerford where she soon produced a welcome hot meal. It was good to tuck in while hearing farming news from Ellis, and telling him all about our day.

The idea was for Jack to have a sleep in a chair during the evening, but I don't think he had much of a sooze even before it was time to say goodbye and let the Bendalls get off to bed.

There was no M1 to speed the journey, and although Colin, Jennifer and I dozed at times, Jack kept driving on. We reached home in time for a few hours' sleep before starting the day's work.

We went to Stamford Bridge station the next day to meet our ponies. They were, of course, quite wild, but were soon coaxed into our trailer before putting them in a loose box at Colin's to be sorted out. Jack somehow managed to get his wrist bashed against the wall in the general melee and cracked a bone, so there was an interval while he went to York to get a plaster fixed.

Later on, all the ponies were turned out in our dale and what a pretty sight they were. They gave us much pleasure and later were broken in and sold. The pretty chestnut went up to the Duchess of Roxburgh and the grey went to Sledmere House. The nightmare drives to Hampshire and back were quite an adventure, and we shall always remember the picnic in the forest at breakfast time.

There is much sadness as well as happiness when you are involved with horses. Jennifer's mare, Lulu, had a beautiful chestnut foal called Coral. Luckily she foaled in the stable and we were there to witness this wonderful sight. So often mares foal quickly when everything is quiet and no-one is around.

One morning a few weeks later Jennifer came panting up to the house from the paddock gasping that the foal was caught up in the wire fence near the dale gate. With wire cutters in hand Jack ran back with her to find a very distressing sight. Poor little Coral was actually hanging almost upside down, caught between strands of wire, but was soon cut free. The vet was called to stitch up the long wound, but the scars always remained.

That year also, Silver Sandals, a specially pretty pony which Maureen loved, and had ridden in shows, was found one Sunday afternoon by a neighbour standing on the daleside with one leg dangling at an alarming angle. There was no alternative but to telephone the Hunt Kennels and have him put down.

At about the same time our dear, faithful old Flicka became so stiff in her joints that she suffered the same fate. She died quickly in her own stable. We have never wished to prolong the lives of any animal which has become too aged and infirm to enjoy life.

Flicka was a great character and it was hard to loose her. She had pulled a grocer's cart in Bridlington before we bought her, and she became greatly loved by all who knew her. She was not a good ride, having a jerky trot, a bumpy canter, not a very good mouth and had no ability in jumping. She carried me for years and was Rachel's first ride as she loved to canter round bareback, charging round the fields Indian-style.

Once, for Bishop Wilton Show we changed the poor pony into an Ayrshire cow for the fancy dress class. Being white with brown patches, she was ideal material, so with horns attached to her bridle

"Ebony" the Shire mare, with foal.

and an udder swinging below, she was led round the ring by a couple of milkmaids with buckets and stools and took a rosette.

Flicka had pulled the old farm float in her younger days and a sledge in snowy weather. She seemed to understand all that was said to her and gave us much pleasure.

During the next few years we lost a young horse with grass sickness and two yearlings with red worm. One of these yearlings was out of a cart mare, Ebony, whom Jack bought for interest and to breed from. She was a good looking mare, but not up to show standard, though we enjoyed one or two attempts at taking her around and even entered her at the Great Yorkshire Show.

Jack's nephew, Edward, took charge there as her groom and slept on the showground. We had to learn the art of getting a heavy horse to show standard. Like all classes of showing, there is a lot of hard work and preparation. Braiding mane and tail, fluffing out those feathery fetlocks, all took time. She was small in the ring compared with those at the top of the line, but it was all an experience. However, someone later wanted to buy her so our venture into shire horses didn't last long.

One weekend, Jack and I went to see a pony we had seen advertised at a little farm near Knaresborough. We were always looking for the perfect pony for one of the girls, and, in any case, I

45

must admit, dealing in a moderate way was Jack's hobby. While he haggled over the price of this pretty pony I looked round the adjoining yard and spied an old stone trough half covered with nettles. Just the thing, I thought, for plants near to our back door. After drawing Jack's attention to the trough, he told the vendor he would do the deal, "But throw the trough in too!"

Before we left, the chap said his wife wanted to know why we wanted the stone trough and when he told her she said, "I wish I had thought of that." We came home, pleased with pony and trough. The latter was long and low like a coffin and very heavy. Such things had not become generally popular when we made that deal. We moved the trough to our retirement home and recently saw one very similar make a hundred pounds in a sale. More than the pony, Cloudy, cost in the 'sixties.

We were constantly rushing off to Horse Trials in which Rachel was having considerable success on Wendy, the sweetest of ponies, quiet enough for me to ride, yet a good performer in Pony Club competitions.

In the spring each year we seldom missed going to the local point-to-points, though racing has never really been of much interest to me. On the odd occasions later when Rachel rode, I admit I was horribly scared.

One had to be fashionable in the 'sixties on such occasions. The tailored suit and shooting stick were essential, though I never had a collection of paddock badges dangling from mine!

One year I was very thrilled with the new clerical grey suit, the 'in' colour, which had two skirts, one straight and the other pleated. I had only worn the favourite 'sun ray' pleated one a few times before getting caught in a heavy storm at Charm Park, a long way from shelter. Alas, the pleats were not permanent as they would be today, and I had to use the suit with the uncomfortable narrow skirt which showed up my hips, which were too ample in any case.

When I bought a suede jacket I felt in the height of fashion, and was holding forth about it at great length when our dear friend, Les, was with us. Being an electrician by trade, he was always keen on new gadgets, and this time he had concealed a tape recorder, his latest toy. I was horrified when the sound of my voice was played back. That awful woman couldn't be me! For years it was a family joke and I was constantly asked how I liked my suede jacket.

CHAPTER 12

Christmas always played a big part in our family life, but I was glad when the actual day arrived as the run-up to it was often hectic. Cards, for instance, and there were masses of them while all the children were at home. I didn't like to display them till Christmas eve and we decided to hang some from the picture rail. Those drawing pin holes are there to this day. Perhaps someone in the future will blame them on the woodworm.

The tree was left till the last minute, and I can hardly think of the lights without a shudder. It was a good idea to have them in a criss-cross chain across the hall and round the large star we hung in the archway, but getting Tony to fix them was another matter. When I did pin him down to tackle the fiddly job, the wretched things wouldn't work so there was much frustration and a swearing session before the illuminations produced the desire effect.

I was usually delighted with the hall when it was finished. We always went to Towthorpe garden for variegated holly, and the evergreens hung from the staircase over the grandfather clock which Mother-in-law had bought from a relation for £7. Brass-faced, with slim mahogony case, it is now greatly treasured.

Sometimes around Christmas, a group of carol singers travelled around the 'tops' as our part of the parish was called and if they came indoors they crowded into the hall to sing for us. That was a traditional Christmas at its best.

The tree was always large and grown on the estate and it, too, often had lights trouble. One Christmas eve morning the girls went to a meet at Kirkham Abbey on ponies and we followed in the Landrover before dashing off to Malton to do some last minute shopping and to exchange presents with relations.

No one was home till five o'clock to do the yard and stable work. There was much to see to indoors too. Tony rushed off to some Young Farmers activities, the sitting room fire was slow to burn and the teleivision conked out!

Poor Jack who was tired, and always ignored the decorating business, sank forlornly into his easy chair muttering, "Blooming rotten Christmas." The girls and I rushed over the jobs of hanging

47

cards and decorating the tree, getting more and more cross. Tony returned at ten o'clock, asking for beans on toast! We all calmed down before going to bed late — and Tony had helped with the lights. I think they worked. There was no midnight church service in our village at that time so we got up early instead for the eight o'clock morning service.

That particular Christmas eve taught us a lesson. Never again did we leave so much to do at the last minute.

We still continued to go to Bridlington for Christmas dinner with mother, stepfather, Lill and perhaps other members of the family. Lill took a great pride in cooking a large turkey and her stuffings and bread sauce were especially good, to say nothing of the rich pudding and rum sauce. Mother came to the fore in carving the bird and wielded the knife in expert fashion. My culinary efforts were delayed till Boxing Day when we returned hospitality and they all descended on us.

In 1961, Maureen was ill on Christmas eve, having complained all day about a pain in her leg which had begun to trouble her at a party the night before. Tony, unusual for him, had retired to bed with a bad attack of 'flu. Next morning neither was any better. We opened all our presents in Maureen's bedroom, huddled round an electric fire, as she was more comfortable lying down.

We worried about leaving her, but I knew everything would be cooking like mad at Bridlington and felt we couldn't disappoint them. We telephoned to explain that there would be two less and our visit would be shorter than usual.

Anxious about our invalids, we returned home as soon as possible and found Tony 'all of a sweat', and poor Maureen in agony. She said she had been listening for ages for the sound of wheels on the gravel.

Our doctor, one of the old school, came out quickly in the midst of his celebrations and prescribed tablets which Jack collected from Pocklington, but admitted that he was mystified by the symptoms. This strange malady caused us great worry and concern, being the first serious illness we had had to cope with. For ten days Jack and I were always on call, day and night, to lift the poor girl to a commode while keeping her legs as straight as possible. When lying still she was cheerful, and had a lot of visitors.

We moved her bed in front of the window and put it on wooden blocks so that she could see out. Laughter, or anyone bumping the

48

bed, caused pain. Sometimes she seemed really poorly and had no appetite. We thought of polio and other diseases. At one stage I read to her during the night as she was so distressed. We were relieved when the doctor sent a specialist to examine her and the following morning I accompanied her in an ambulance to the City Hospital.

It seemed dreadful to leave the fifteen-year-old in an adult ward, and I felt quite devastated as I walked around York carrying her day clothes till it was time to catch a bus back home.

From that day, for five weeks, we visited the hospital daily. Jennifer, being at home, was a great help, but it was an extremely worrying period, with little information from doctors or hospital staff. There were various tests, and the talk of moving Maureen to Leeds. No one seemed to understand the illness. Luckily a pleasant woman in the next bed befriended Maureen, and many friends and relations rallied round to visit. I really think the most acute stage was over before the specialist saw her, and gradually her condition improved without treatment.

One never to be forgotten evening we found her sitting up in bed, and from that time she gradually learned to walk again. We were lucky that the winter was mild as never once was there any difficulty on journeys to York. Then came the great day in February when we brought her home and had a celebration meal. After all, she had missed her Christmas dinner!

Maureen had a whole term off school, and it was summer before she could run and forget the lame leg. The summing up of the case was vague. As far as we could understand, an unusual virus had affected the nerves in her thigh which needed time to grow again.

CHAPTER 13

Farming patterns were gradually changing, though the hand picking of taties lasted through the 'sixties which had started off with a bad season with the last being lifted on December 6th 1960. I was so pleased to be sending out the last 'looance that I baked mince pies as a celebration.

We had some late harvests 'finished combining'. October 13th was one example. In 1963 we increased our acreage by taking over the tenancy of Manna Green, a small farm which adjoined Cot Nab land. The previous tenant had died and this farm of a hundred-and-thirty-five acres, with a poor house and buildings situated down a long narrow lane, was ideal to join on to Cot Nab. A good part of it was rough grazing in a dale similar to ours.

We often wondered at the origin of the name of the farm. Perhaps mushrooms once grew in profusion, like manna? Unlike most wold farms, Manna Green had no shelter belt, and the farmstead faced the elements unprotected. In days gone by it would have been thought a lonely spot, and was the first place to get snowed up as the lane drifted in after the slightest fall.

When Jennifer was at Studley College she came home for half term in a winter when we had more snow than usual. Great drifts overhung the dale like cliffs and we could walk over some of the five bar gates. Sheep were a worry and had to be brought into the shelter of the paddock.

When Jennifer went back to Warwickshire, other students could not believe the snowy condition she described. We found this with Pocklington friends, as the wolds were another world when blizzards raged, changing the whole landscape. Quite often we had motorists temporarily stranded in our kitchen, sometimes because of snow or if their car had skidded off the road on ice, and sometimes because they required a mechanic.

Once, our neighbours, the Pauls, were given a bed when, after following us back from a dance at Stamford Bridge, they knew there was no hope of getting through the snow down Malton road to their lane. Another time, we were woken in the early hours by two chaps we knew whose car had stuck in drifts. They had battled with the

Calves in the dale.

elements to reach us and spent the rest of the night in armchairs in front of an electric fire.

At all times of the year motorists used to arrive at the back door asking for a bucket of water for a boiling radiator. Cars in those days were not as good on Garrowby Hill. These constant requests could be quite a nuisance, and when gardening I would fill a bucket and leave it at the back door. If someone walked down the drive, leaving a car on the roadside, I would just call out, "There's a bucket of water at the back door". The motorists always looked very surprised. I expect they all thought their plight was unusual.

We got used to calming people down after accidents which were more frequent before the road was straightened and improved, giving us a wide grass verge. I was accustomed to dialling '999', though at first found myself all shaky. The sight of a motorcyclist lying on the road with a bloody face really worried me, but I stayed with him till help came, and later he wrote to thank me.

We had a group of people, two of whom were known to us, in the kitchen one icy morning after two cars had collided. We were more concerned for the pregnant lady and her friend who had a nasty cut on her head, than a man who seemed dazed but unharmed. The ambulance took them all to hospital and we were astounded to hear that the poor man had collapsed and died soon after being admitted.

One lady with a broken down car asked to use the 'phone one evening and I heard her say, "Eeh, no, I don't know wherever I am, but it's right out in the wilds!" She later asked whatever we found to do, living in such a lonely place. I expect she thought we never went anywhere and just sat around vegetating.

One July afternoon we returned from Driffield Show to the astonishing spectacle of a cabin cruiser resting on top of our high garden hedge. Underneath it was a Landrover and trailer. We quickly made enquiries about this strange phenomenon and found it was a 'Daily Express' Show Boat which toured coastal resorts as the basis for fashion parades.

Unfortunately for Jack, the fashion models had gone on by car, but the boat was full of valuable clothes, so had to be carefully guarded. The driver admitted he must have dozed off and lost control while taking the bend in the road. After making 'phone calls, he ended up being fed in our kitchen as he had been warned to stay near the boat. He also spent the night perched up on the hedge in the cabin, guarding the clothes!

52

The Daily Express showboat being lifted from the garden hedge.

After breakfast, for which he abandoned his perch, a small crane arrived to lift the boat. Of course we took photographs and later said goodbye to our visitor. As far as I can remember, there was no compensation for this unexpected visitor, or damage to the hedge, but Jack soon remedied that with the help of the ever useful binder twine.

Thinking of unexpected visitors, the biggest influx descended on us in the early hours of a cold autumn night in the 'seventies. We were awakened by someone calling under our bedroom window. Jack sprang out of bed to find a policeman in the garden asking for shelter for a coachload of trippers returning from Blackpool illuminations. They had got more 'illumination' on the homeward journey when, close to our farm, the coach burst into flames!

Luckily, everyone got out in time, but imagine how they felt, after being half or fully asleep and then having to huddle against the wall of our buildings. The policeman asked if they could find better shelter in the covered yard. I hurriedly threw on some clothes and followed him round to the waiting crowd and invited them all into the house.

Jack also dressed, and we switched on the fan heater in the kitchen and lit the dining room fire, as there were about forty people including some young children. Maureen was living in the cottage at that time and, hearing the hullabaloo, also got up and helped me make tea for our nocturnal party.

We got out toys for the children and soon everyone was relaxed, with kiddies running up and down the hall. Ladies helped to wash up mugs and cups, luckily we had a lot, and chattered about their experience. They were with us for an hour or more before a relief coach arrived. They were very grateful, but we had been glad to help and I later received a beautiful bouquet from the stranded trippers.

Another experience resulting from being a roadside farm took place when Rachel was about seventeen and alone in the house one evening when we were down in the village for a harvest supper.

Early picture of the farm buildings before alterations.

54

She had had a bath and put on a nightie and dressing gown when her dog wanted to go outside. On letting Zelda out, she noticed a light go on in the far buildings. Feeling rather worried, she grabbed the dog by the collar and marched towards the light calling out, "Who's there?"

A youngish chap appeared, explaining that he was tramping around, and could she cook some bacon for him? Rachel answered, "I can't cook. You'd better come in and do it yourself." So he followed her to the kitchen with bacon in hand and she produced frying pan, fat, eggs and bread.

At this moment Colin Newlove 'phoned to talk to Jack. "And what are you doing?" he asked. "Oh, I'm entertaining a tramp," she replied. In typical fashion, Colin jumped into his car and walked into the kitchen to find, as he later told us, "This scruffy chap sitting at the table eating bacon and eggs, and Rachel perched near him in her nightgown!"

The man was questioned by Colin and escorted back to the barn with instructions not to smoke. He told them he had had a spell in the navy, but preferred the open road to the sea.

We arrived back to hear of this rather alarming episode, but Rachel insisted she could tell he was harmless, and the only worrying part had been walking towards the light not knowing who was there. Jack went out to have a word with our lodger before bedtime, and he was off on his way early the next morning, without bacon for breakfast, no doubt!

The dog Zelda was not with us for long. A cross-bred Alsatian, we thought she had been thrown from a car as Rachel found her wandering forlornly on the roadside and adopted her as her own dog. Unfortunately we soon found she had mange which proved to be the worse possible kind.

In spite of many visits to the vet, ointments and other treatments, the poor bitch became such a pitiful sight that in the end had to be put out of her misery.

CHAPTER 14

Early in the 'sixties, the Estate decided to retile our long hall. I was very fond of the old Victorian tiles with their geometrical patterns in muted colours, but they had been loose in parts when we had arrived at Cot Nab and we kept solving the problem by strategically placed rugs. All the same, we kept picking up loose fragments, and it was rapidly approaching the impossible stage.

A wood block floor would have looked wonderful, but it cost too much, so we settled for terrazzo tiles in shades of grey. We usually had to pay a portion of the costs for such improvements, and this type of tile was quite expensive.

There was, of course, a great state of chaos in the house with all parts difficult, if not impossible, to reach during various stages of the work. I loaded a trolley, an old strong oak one bought by my mother in the 'thirties, with everything I thought I would need from the dairy before the men arrived, in order to avoid crossing the back section near the kitchen. It also meant going round the garden to the front door to use the loo, or to make a telephone call.

We balanced on planks to reach the stairs and various other hazards cropped up before it was all finished. It looked very clean and tidy, but lacked the warmer look of the old tiles. We missed the clattering for some time, too.

Around that time, our old Yorkist range was taken out and a simple brick fireplace built in its place, the grate having a back boiler. This made the room look much better. After all, it was used as a dining room as well as a kitchen, and we spent much time there. The big table seated twelve. We found a lovely piece of old oak for a mantlepiece. The deep sink had already gone, also those tiresome doors, and I now had a stainless steel double-drainer, much to my delight.

In the dining room, where our old mahogany chairs had begun to collapse and the big table needed repair, we had an Acorn sideboard and four chairs in oak. Tony visited Brandsby Acorn Industries with the Young Farmers and came back with an ashtray as a present for me saying, "This is where you should go for dining room stuff."

In due course we did go to look round and ended up by ordering

56

the good, solid oak hand crafted furniture, though it meant waiting a long time, and longer to save up for it!

I tried to keep the kitchen tidy as all callers came through that door, and there were a lot of them some days, 'reps' as well as tradesmen. Near the door stood the old mahogany dresser which was always littered with something or other. It was far too handy as a dumping place for whatever anyone in the family was carrying as they came in or in passing to and from the hall. Daily I cleared up a little, but often got into trouble for moving things. "Where is that screwdriver I put here the other day?" "Have you seen the syringe? I know I put it in the bowl here." That bowl was constantly filled with oddments, though its use was intended to be purely ornamental. Caps, riding sticks and dandy brushes all had temporary resting places there. Letters waiting for the post, bills to be paid, newspaper and farm magazines, all had their corner at the back, but the pile often got so high it was in danger of overbalancing.

The original kitchen curtains had gone into holes as the windows got full sun for much of the day, that is, when we were not shrouded in mist, common to the high wolds, and I asked Mother-in-law to make new ones. The material was very up to date, with a bold design

Neurotic dog "Printer" in garden pond.

57

of cooks and chefs in rows. Unfortunately I am hopeless at arithmetic and measurements and had a 'phone call from her one evening asking, "Are you sure you have measured these curtains right. They do seem long." "Oh, yes," I said, "Seven feet, three and a half yards, that's OK." Luckily Jack was listening and put the matter to rights, but I have never heard the end of it!

We had so much leftover material that Mother-in-law machined several aprons to sell at the church sale and also made a curtain for the old boot rack in the lobby. This actually came in useful later when Rachel had a very neurotic spaniel called Printer who disliked being left alone in a room. One evening we were out for a short time leaving him in the kitchen. We returned to find plant pots from the window sills all over the floor, and one curtain hanging in shreds as far as he had been able to reach. At least we had matching material to use for repairs!

For a few months, one summer in the mid 'sixties, we had a rather strange family in the cottage. Their name was Polish and unpronounceable, so I will just call them Boris and Beryl. She came from Berkshire and had a soft southern accent. They had four lovely children, the youngest only a few months old. Boris was a likeable chap, very polite, willing and anxious to please. Beryl was far too plump, but had a sweet smile. She was mostly very placid and easy going, and although loving her children dearly, was totally unfussy and lacking in hygiene. Despite this they were all extremely healthy.

They had little in the way of possessions, so we went to a local auction sale for a carpet or two and various pieces of furniture which were received with great joy. The little girls played with toys, dolls and prams from our storeroom and we soon became fond of them. They all, in fact, seemed happy to be next door.

Boris was limited as to what work he could do and hadn't a driving licence which was a disadvantage, though he was proud to own a moped. We soon discovered, however, that all was not as it appeared.

Boris was subject to sudden fits of depression and temper during which he seemed to lose control of his senses. We found it difficult to understand the first time, when he suddenly left his work in the fields and galloped towards home, shouting and waving his arms.

Beryl was in our kitchen at the time, saw him from the window and turned to me with her pretty face full of fear. "Oh, missus," she said, "Boris is having one of his turns," and rushed off, gathering up the children as she went back to her cottage. We heard much ranting and raving then saw him storming off alone up the road.

Later, he returned, and tried to explain in his halting English that he was a good Catholic, but a sinner because his marriage to Beryl wasn't right in the eyes of God. She had been married before and only the younger children were his, so she was a 'bad woman'. His fixation about this spilled over without control whenever a car parked near the cottage and he was certain it belonged to one of her lovers! These suspicions only arose if one of his strange moods was upon him.

However, this first episode passed and we thought little of it until the next unbalanced period descended on poor Boris. Some said it coincided with phases of the moon, some that it was the after effects of being badly treated as a prisoner of war, but the next time it happened we were quite alarmed.

Beryl called at our doorway one morning in tears. "Come, misses, come. Boris is smashing up the furniture." I went round and found such a pitiful scene, with the children wide-eyed and crying, and Boris wielding a hammer over the table. I shouted at him and also burst into tears while comforting Beryl. This brought him quickly to his senses. "Missus, I do anything for you. I do not want you like this,", and on one knee he took my hand and kissed it. Then he stalked out of the house, got on his moped and wasn't seen for two days.

Poor Beryl was frightened at the thought of his return. We kept the communicating upstairs door to the cottage unlocked and I gave her a large poker to keep by her bed. Boris came rampaging back one afternoon and on seeing him, Beryl and the three children ran into our house. I was fastening the door when she exclaimed, "Oh, the baby, missus, I've left the baby." "Don't worry," I said, grabbing a walking stick from the porch, "I'll get the baby".

Just as I turned a corner, I bumped into Jack. "Here," I said, giving him the stick, "You go to Boris and rescue the baby." Following at a safe distance I entered the cottage to find poor Boris on his knees, clasping a crucifix to his chest. "Don't worry, missus". Then, turning to Jack he said, "You can put the stick down. I won't hurt my baby".

However he was in such a frantic state, and we couldn't keep on harbouring his family, so Jack 'phoned the police and Boris was taken off, clutching his radio under one arm. Like many people with mental problems, he could quickly become rational and plausible when cornered. In hospital he discharged himself and, once more, arrived back with Beryl and the children.

By this time we had decided that we could no longer cope, and to our surprise Boris was given a job on a farm in North Yorkshire without us being asked for references. We bade them a sad farewell. They were such a tragic family for whom we could see little hope in the future.

We visited them at Christmas in their new home and took gifts for the children, but, alas, we soon heard they were on the move once more.

CHAPTER 15

Like most teenagers of the 'sixties, Rachel and her schoolfriends became mad about the Beatles. Photographs of them were avidly collected and raved over, with Paul the favourite. We were spared constant record playing, not having a gramophone, as I would call it, in the house.

However, daughters have a way of getting round their fathers, and, with the help of four friends to back her up, Rachel persuaded Jack to take them to see their heroes at a pop concert in Leeds, which coincided with the half term holiday. Another father managed to get the precious tickets. Jack felt very apprehensive about letting himself in for all this, having heard and read so much about the dreadful, screaming youngsters who made nuisances of themselves at such concerts up and down the country.

This sort of outing was not in my line and Jack felt he needed some support in his role of protector, so was well pleased when his old friend Les, a good-natured bachelor, volunteered to accompany the party, which, after meeting at our house, set off for Leeds.

I waited anxiously for the return. Two friends were to stay the night with us, and two were being taken home en route. I have seldom seen Jack so overcome by an experience either before or since. He couldn't stop talking about the immense crowds, the ear-shattering noise, and how fearful they had been of getting crushed or bowled over in the mob.

The girls said it had all been super, but they were somewhat disappointed because they had heard so little because of the screaming audience. They had hoped to listen, but no chance, although the mere sight of the FOUR had made their evening worthwhile.

The build-up to the high spot of the programme had been tedious, but once the Beatles appeared, "All hell was let loose," as Jack said, and "No-one would credit it, without actually being there". Some kids fainted and all stood up to shriek themselves hoarse, or were restrained by the police from trying to reach the stage, some to throw the inevitable jelly babies.

Jack and Les really seemed to get more excitement out of the visit than the girls, who couldn't stop grumbling about the behaviour of that mass of hysterical kids, and to this day Jack enjoys telling his story of "The night I went to a Beatles concert".

As our family grew older and started going places and 'courting', to use an outdated word, we decided to stop worrying about what time they came home and merely left a list of the four names on the kitchen table as we went to bed. These were duly crossed off, and the last one home locked the back door. We weren't so security conscious then. Sometimes, of course, we were also out gallivanting, so our names were put on the list, too, though it seldom happened that we were all out together in different places. The dances and hunt balls continued to be popular and we frequently travelled around the local towns or villages, joining up with friends and other members of the Megginson clan.

In 1962 I volunteered to go to the AGM of the W.I. at the Albert Hall and, in my usual way, tried to fit in too many other activities at the same time. A new vicar and family were about to move into the vicarage after Mr. Fawcett's long incumbency of over twenty years. Much redecorating had been done, but not the larder. So, to ease the worries of the new vicar's wife, I offered to paint the ceiling and walls which I finished late one evening before rushing off the next morning to visit my old school friend Pam and husband Roy in Beckenham for a night before starting my official duties as delegate.

All went well, and the next morning I thought I was quite clever to find my way to the Albert Hall in good time. So good in fact there was no one else there, and the doors were shut. "Well," I thought, "All these thousands of women and I am the first to arrive." I went for a walk in Kensington Gardens before returning to those handsome portals, but there was still a deserted look about the place. I saw a poster and, with pounding heart, had to admit to myself that I was a day LATE.

Never will I forget that moment. My heart literally plummetted to my best summer sandals while I slowly wandered away. Gradually I recovered my senses, and bought a postcard to send to our president. I sat on a bench in the nearby park, took out my pen and wrote my apologies. The post was quicker in those days and I thought, "Well, that's that. I'm in the capital city and have to amuse myself until it's time to return to Beckenham."

I went round Harrods and then to a matinee performance of 'Boeing-Boeing' before returning to tell Pam, Roy and their children of my stupid mistake. They, of course, thought it all a great joke.

I couldn't give a report to our W.I. but I made up for my shortcomings by inviting them all up to Cot Nab on a fine, sunny evening, where we had a happy party with supper indoors after games of tennis for the more energetic. Others were content to stroll in the garden or sit and enjoy the view down the dale.

That is an episode I have never lived down and to this day whenever any meeting is arranged I am told, "Be sure you go on the right day!"

CHAPTER 16

We now became involved in such important family occasions as twenty-first parties and weddings. Two 'coming of age' parties, thank goodness there were no 'eighteenths' too, for Tony and Maureen, were held at home with games around the house and dancing in the kitchen. The big table was, with some difficulty, carried out to the garage, to make a clear space, and Les rigged up some music. Being an electrician, Uncle Les, as the children called him, was helpful on all such occasions. Sadley Les died far too young, and we miss him very much.

Tony must have been smartly dressed for his party as it was worth recording in the diary that he bought a "very expensive suit — £27".

Jennifer married Derek when only twenty and her party was shared with a friend and held in the same shed as the wedding. A

Irene, Jack and Mother-in-law at a family wedding in 1963.

shed seems a strange place to hold such important functions, but this shed was brand new at the time and of the Crendon Concrete variety. It covered an area formerly occupied by a small fold yard with little pig or calf boxes opening off, and was conveniently situated near the house and outside loo.

The wedding was planned for July and after going into the costs of marquees on hire, we decided to make the new shed as pretty as possible. For weeks beforehand we made pink cherry blossom flowers from tissue paper and wired them on to bare branches. Nearer the day we brought in great boughs of larch from the wood.

When the day arrived it all looked very attractive, with hired tables and chairs. A group of very capable ladies from the village came up to help with the refreshments which were mostly home made, but also included trays of little cakes and fancies collected from a firm in York. We catered for two hundred guests, and provided the carved buffet for the evening ourselves with help from friends. Jack was very keen that we should have a dance in the evening and we got a good local band to play.

Somehow, amid last minute preparations for all this, we found time to attend another Garrowby party, this time to celebrate Lord Irwin's coming of age. We did have to leave a little early as our weekend guests were already arriving before we got home.

I remember being on my knees in front of the oven taking out sausages when people had started leaving for the church. However, all went well on this happy day.

Looking back, that summer seems to have been rather a nightmare period, in as much as there was so much extra work to fit in. I helped with the decoration of the little cottage where Jennifer and Derek would live and, of course, there was all the extra shopping which a wedding involves.

In the middle of all this, my mother's health began to fail. My stepfather had died and Lill found it too difficult to cope with Mother unaided, although Lill herself was still very active. We eventually decided to move them both into our cottage which, fortunately, became free after the occupants agreed to move to Manna Green, not minding either the loneliness or the dilapidated state of the house.

There was a lot of work in cleaning the cottage and making it cosy for Mother and Lill. Mother would have her bed downstairs, so an alarm bell was fixed, and various alterations made. All the furniture

Irene's mother in her old age, with "Doddy", a friend who often visited us.

had to be moved from Bridlington, some to be shared round the family, and arrangements made for the house to be sold. All this to be done before the wedding!

But, we coped, and everyone pulled together to achieve this removal which meant we were glad to have family next door where we could keep an eye on them and I was able to share the caring for Mother, whom we pushed from one house to another in a wheel chair. She was glad to have our company, and Lill could have a little peace. Also, Lill helped me with cooking jobs as they ate their main meals with us.

Maureeen, who had trained as a nursery nurse, married David when she was twenty-one and that wedding took place at a difficult time, too, as Mother died between sending out invitations and the actual wedding day.

Mother had become practically bedridden with Lill and I taking turns to sleep in her room for many months. It was distressing to watch this very lively and strong personality gradually losing all faculties and becoming so cabbage-like.

For Maureen's autumn wedding we had about a hundred guests in the house, and for the special day the big table was again moved out and the kitchen filled with small tables. We disguised the sink and cooker with potted plants which we had hired for the occasion, a very useful inspiration as they could be spread around the whole house, yet took no time to arrange.

Both rooms also had small tables, and drinks were served from the dairy. With Mother's room free, we moved in there for the day and used that kitchen too. The hall became very congested during the reception, and when the cake was cut and speeches made around the sideboard, there were guests crowded in all directions and half way up the stairs. In the evening we took a large prarty to the 'Three Cups' at Stamford Bridge for a meal.

The years which followed were very much easier for me, personally, as dear old Lill was so contented in the cottage alone. She could do as she liked with her home, for the first time in her life, no longer having a boss.

Lill (and "Dinah") bring the dustbin from the drive gate.

For me it was a wonderful period as Lill came through to help me each morning with cooking, baking and perhaps some housework. She started making bread again, and her buns were popular with callers. She also loved the garden and worked hard in her little patch.

The great thing was that she could look after the dogs, and was around if I went away or even off for a day. We took her with us shopping or on drives out, and having always had a great love of the countryside, it was a joy for her to live in the midst of it.

I felt free to go off to painting classes or other activities with friends, or to horsey events with Rachel. I could leave home for a few days knowing that Jack and Tony would be well fed and everything would be in apple-pie order.

It is strange how life's pattern works out. Lill had been like a nanny to me when young, in spite of having most of the household tasks to fit in as well. Then, in my difficult days as a young farm wife, she came two days a week by bus to help me, so I was glad to give her the comfort and support she needed when her health failed.

By the time she was limited to living in one room, Maureen had become a single parent with three little girls, so they took over the ever valuable cottage and Lill was moved into one of our spare rooms. She contentedly passed the days knitting or reading in a chair in front of a window which looked out to garden, dale and farm yard.

The grandchildren gave her pleasure and Maureen was a great help as a "Lill-sitter" and, towards the end, shared the nursing when this tough old lady finally passed from this world in 1978.

CHAPTER 17

This was also a period of helping to decorate houses for Jennifer and Maureen. I could easily go off for the day to lend a hand in this direction. Jennifer's second home provided some surprises with funny nooks and crannies. It had been unoccupied for some time so was in a poor state. In fact, birds had nested inside and rats had eaten part of the electric cables.

When stripping paper off the walls of a deep upstairs cupboard which we felt could have originally been a powder closet in the days when men powdered their hair, we discovered the walls had, at one time, been papered with pages from "Weldon Ladies Journal". There they were, in all their glory, Edwardian ladies so beautifully

Jack on "Ronaldsway", and Irene on "Wendy", all woolly in winter coat.

arrayed in costumes of the period, softly coloured and such a pity to destroy. We carefully removed some undamaged pages to put away or to frame.

This house had the original iron fireplaces which looked lovely when in use. I say "original", but I am probably quite wrong, as parts of the building were obviously of the period when open hearths would burn large logs.

By now, we had grandchildren who didn't exactly help in the painting and decorating department. The little girls were a great joy to us and Jack, crooning over the side of Sally's carrycot when she was about six weeks old was heard to say, "And we'll have to get a little pony for you before long, won't we?"

Sure enough, only months later, he came home from a sale with Gollywog, a sweet black shaggy Shetland. As soon as Sally was old enough she was lifted on to his back and yet another little girl became horse mad.

Rachel was, by the late 'sixties, still spending much of her life in the saddle, having taken an exam course as assistant instructor in Lancashire. She dutifully did the farm secretarial training, as a safeguard we insisted, before taking various horsey jobs, helping on the farm, or travelling round the countryside competing in one-day events or in showjumping classes.

She was well placed in Pony Club and Riding Club championships on her beloved horse, Ronaldsway, and also won novice sections in official horse trials.

Sometimes I was the best groom available, as Jack was often too busy to leave the farm, but for the more important three day events a more efficient helper was found, sometimes Suzanne Mason, who would travel with her.

We often had adventures on our journeys around England. Perched high in the cab of the old horse box we had good views of the countryside, for Rachel had no qualms about driving this old lorry, actually called "Annie Lorry" with its precious load.

Tempers were frayed on many occasions, what with competition nerves, the worry of the horse's condition and sometimes getting lost on the outskirts of a city or having trouble negotiating a difficult, narrow gateway to a stable yard. I learned to sit tight and keep quiet.

There was no radio so I sometimes relieved the monotony of long motorway journeys by reading aloud to the driver. We found children's classics as good as any books for this, but once, after a

70

Rachel drives "Annie Lorry".

specially successful day, we almost dissolved in tears over "Black Beauty".

We often slept in the lorry and this was far from luxurious. No bunks, no cooker or sink, no loo, as found in top class horse boxes. We first saw to Ronnie's comfort, and he always had good stable accommodation, then we mucked out the lorry floor and left it to air.

Accommodation varied from a small private stable to elegant stud farms with clock tower, potted plants, beds of geraniums and much gleaming white paint. Once we had quarters in a race course stables where we slept on iron bedsteads usually intended for jockeys.

Always I cooked on a tiny picnic stove in a corner of "Annie Laurie". This was difficult after dark as we only had a battery lamp, but there were usually competitors nearby to meet up with, and the horse to be fussed over. I only did such menial jobs as rolling bandages for the legs and tail, or leading the precious animal around to graze or when cooling off.

Once, the lorry was parked at Chatsworth and I was thrilled with the beautiful surroundings. There were good loos, too, and a hot breakfast available for competitors and grooms.

Sometimes we were especially lucky and could stay with our Wiltshire farming friends. Ellis and Margery were keen on horses,

71

too, and we were certain of a good welcome from their family as well. Tidworth and Wylie were important events, within easy reach of their farm. No cooking to do, and comfortable beds instead of sleeping bags on straw. One could never get rid of the "pong" in the lorry. I even shook talcum powder on the pillow, but I still kept wrinkling my nostrils as pungent whiffs rose from the floor boards.

Like all competitors at all levels of this sport, there were high spots for the rider and low ones too. Once, after a clear cross country round at Burghley, Rachel took the wrong course in the show jumping and was thus eliminated. A controversial technical refusal put her down a place at Tidworth and at Badminton, on her first attempt there, the worst tragedy of all happened. Dear Ronaldsway met his death jumping water, after going splendidly for three-quarters of the course.

That afternoon will remain in our memories for ever. The absolute devastion for us, and more so for Rachel and Suzanne who had to leave for the long drive home with an empty horse box. The kindness of good friends who were with us will remain. We tried to

Rachel has a clear cross-country round on "Ronaldsway" at Burghley.

72

forget our grief by staying another night as planned. Afterwards, complete strangers as well as many friends wrote to offer sympathy which was a help and the BBC even gave Rachel their film of that fatal round as far as the last jump. Recovery from the shock took some time, but another good horse was found and ridden successfully. But none of those who followed on over the years was quite as loved by us all as poor Ronaldsway.

One travel experience is still vivid in my mind. We were returning from horse trials in the south with Torridon and Tregembo in the lorry. It was a cold, wet day, and the wind was blowing through the floorboards. In an attempt to counteract this, Rachel had strapped a pair of the horses' brushing boots on her ankles over her trousers.

Somewhere in the region of Ashby-de-la-Zouch, the clutch on the lorry went and we came to a halt. With much cursing, Rachel jumped down from the cab and went running off along the hardcore of the M1 to find the nearest telephone. Although I was worried, I had to smile at the strange sight of her booted ankles as viewed from behind. She returned, all wet, to say the breakdown truck would soon be with us and, sure enough, it wasn't long in arriving.

Rachel was most concerned about being towed, chiefly for fear of jogging the precious animals in the back, and Torridon wasn't ours. However there was no alternative but to follow our leader to the garage a few miles from the motorway. There, the lorry was pulled over an inspection pit. The rain still poured down and one chap called to the other, "You'll need your wellies on if you're going down there," to which Rachel replied, "You'll need your umbrella, too, if the horses want a pee!" A natural reaction when coming to a halt after long hours of travelling.

I was shown to an office to telephone home and to huddle over a little electric fire while Rachel saw to the horses, and later went off with the mechanic for a trial run.

"Why do you go round the country in a clapped out lorry?" he asked. "Well," said Rachel, "I'd rather go round in a clapped out lorry and have good horses than have a smart box with clapped out horses!" Both had been successful in the three day event at Tidworth.

We were late home that evening, needless to say, but arrived at last, safe and sound, but tired and hungry.

73

CHAPTER 18

In the summer of 'sixty-five, we had the great joy of welcoming for the day coachloads of children from a school in Hull. The headmistress, Avril, was a friend, and when she called to see us she remarked how much she would like her children from Buckingham Street school to see what a farm and our sort of countryside looked like. They were not deprived children in one sense of the word, and not lacking in material things, but they had little knowledge of any environment other than their somewhat sordid surroundings in central Hull.

So it was all arranged. They would come to us rather than the usual seaside trip and learn a little about what life on the farm was all about. Avril arrived, supported by her staff, and soon had the eighty children well in control and then divided them into separate groups.

The hills were a great novelty, and as one child had said during the journey, he didn't think he would want to go up a hill in case he fell off, it was obviously a new landscape for them to encounter.

One batch of excited kiddies streamed off across the paddock, sending the two ponies into a frightened state. I shouted to the teachers to get the children into a bunch and to stand still while I got help to catch the galloping ponies and bring them into the stable.

The party then proceeded to the dale where they caused the staff a few anxious moments by running downhill too fast with resulting tumbles. However, no one was hurt. Another group explored the wood, gathered hemlock, picked up larch cones and ended by playing Red Indians, while another was taken round the yard to see poultry, pigs and calves. The two pet lambs were very popular.

The sight of piglets clinging to the sow's teats brought the exclamation, "Look at that lot snoggin!" from one excited little boy, and the muscovy ducks with the comical faces amused them. One duck had nested in the garden hedge, and the children formed a quiet queue to peer through a little gap to see the mother sitting on her nest of fifteen eggs.

A queue also formed for those anxious to experience a pony ride. Jennifer came to help in this venture, and Tony took charge of a

74

Buckingham Street children with flowers and horse-shoe.

tractor-trailer drive round fields behind the wood. Straw bales round the trailer sides helped to keep the children safe on this little expedition.

The picnic lunch was eaten in the garden and fortunately the weather was warm enough to sit in orderly circles on the lawn. We provided cups of tea for the adults and plastic beakers of orange squash for the children. Serving the latter was rather like taking part in a relay race as we seemed to constantly refill the empty beakers and then dash back for more.

Colin Newlove kindly brought his Ayrshire bull, Taurus, to entertain them with a display on the lawn. I very much doubt if any of the children realised the trust and patience required to get a young bull to perform such tricks as lying down to order while Colin leaned against him to read a newspaper, or to balance on a plank, to say nothing of the "Give us a kiss" routine.

My mother, brought out to the garden in her wheelchair, was greatly charmed by the kiddies and they were fascinated by her. A

75

Colin Newlove takes a bow on the performing bull.

small group seemed to mill around her chair constantly, and even offered little bunches of buttercups. They loved the freedom of running around the field and wood, gathering cow parsley ('umlocks' in our dialect), ferns and daisies.

Before they left I took a few older girls round the house — really to jump the queue for the outside toilet — and found them very interested, especially in the bedrooms. They seemed to think our house a mansion compared with the ones in Hull which they described to me.

I found some old horse shoes which I gave to a few who came running up on seeing them, and was soon besieged with requests, "Please, miss, can I have one?" They gathered up a strange collection of souvenirs, wilting flowers, sheep's wool, feathers and larch cones.

The little ones looked weary by the time they left us, and I expect they would fall asleep on the coach. We waved them off, wondering what tales they would have to tell on reaching home. What with mountains and forests, the performing bull and being chased by horses, I'm sure there would be some unbelieving parents.

A few weeks later, Avril brought us a wonderful collection of letters and beautiful drawings which gave us an insight into how we

76

and the farm had impressed the town children. They included expressions such as "playing in the forest" and a picture of "the farmer 'arvesting his corn". Another, "the farmer's wife feeding hens", showed me wearing a gold lamé dress, a wonderful bit of applique work! Several letters and pictures referred to the "old lady in the wheelchair".

It was a rewarding experience for us, and we shall remember with joy the day the children came.

CHAPTER 19

The Highways Department had at last recognised the danger of the bend in the road near our wood and farmyard, so there was a great invasion of people and road work machinery. The result was a straight road and a much wider grass verge with a lay-by beyond the wood. This was a great improvement and we were now unlikely to have accident victims in the kitchen or cabin cruisers on the garden hedge!

Just before the road scheme started, local archaeologists were permitted to dig on the opposite side of Garrowby Street, opposite Cot Nab, and close to the line of entrenchments on South Wold farm. To their great excitement, they unearthed a skeleton, described as a 'freak' specimen, some four thousand years old. Mr. T.C. Brewster, the Ministry Archaeologist who conducted the excavations of the two Bronze Age burial mounds, said the skeleton was found underneath a mound dating between 1800 and 2400 BC. The unusual skull shape proclaimed it to be a freak.

We, of course, rushed along to see this remarkable discovery and took photographs of this early resident of the Wolds. Mr. Brewster made much use of our telephone and before long the poor freak's bones were carefully packed up and sent to the Natural History Museum.

Later that year, the pump in our dairy caused us quite a lot of trouble and for a few days our water supply was cut off. We could use the outside toilet, and carry in water from the sink nearby, but life was somewhat difficult.

In the middle of all this, I had to organise a funeral party, as an elderly ex-vicar of our parish had died in Kirkbymoorside, and he wished to be buried in Bishop Wilton church yard alongside other priests of St. Edith's. His wife and daughters had been good friends to us, so I was glad to offer hospitality after the funeral service. I was, however, worried about our lack of toilet facilities, especially as the Bishop would be with us. I felt I could hardly direct him through the back passage to the somewhat sordid loo.

Tony came to the rescue at the last minute by rigging up a complicated contraption with various pipes from the storage tank in

78

the garden behind the house, leading up to the bathroom window, then dangling in loops through the loft to the household tank. We were saved. Chains pulled again, and taps gushed, but after all this, would you believe it, His Grace didn't need to go!

Some time before this, the storage tank in the loft had been left uncovered and a mouse, or it could have been mice, had ventured in and been drowned. We knew nothing of this till our cold water taps seized up. The plumber was called and, to our horror, found the cause of the blockage to be the partially decomposed body of a very dead mouse. We shuddered to think of the water we had drunk in the last few days, but no one suffered any ill effects. After that, a new cover was put on the tank.

By the late 'sixties, Rachel was down in Devon working for Bertie Hill, the top trainer and Olympic Gold medalist. She had a lot of good rides on various horses, and sometimes had her own down there too.

We took a week's holiday, and I loved not only meeting her friends, but seeing Devon again, and had a nostalgic day driving round the area around Dartmoor where I had worked as a pre-war girl groom. We had much fun with the crowd from Bertie's, watching a training session or two and went to spectate at a one day event at Farleigh Castle when Rachel was competing.

That autumn, while Rachel was still in Devon, we had the excitement of our first trip to Europe. Jack had never been keen to travel and refused to fly anywhere, but he couldn't resist the chance to see Rachel competing in Holland, so braved the North Sea ferry and overcame his reluctance to drive on the wrong side of the road. He thoroughly enjoyed coping with the various hazards and language difficulties, though most people spoke some English. We hated the night at sea, deep in the bowels of the ferry near the juddering engines, but it was all a novelty, as was the long drive to Deurne, through the flat countryside.

The equestrian centre where the event was held was very grand and there we met Rachel and the other British riders who had crossed the Channel from Harwich with their horse boxes. We were soon walking the cross country course, over woodland tracks on sandy soil where the oak trees had extra large leaves in astonishingly bright autumn colours.

Over the years we must have walked a hundred miles or more round cross country courses, examining jumps and giving ourselves

79

heart failure at the thought of our daughter and our horse trying to successfully negotiate seemingly impossible obstacles. This time it was in kilometres and the twisting course was one which needed a good memory and concentration to avoid getting lost. I always got butterflies listening to commentaries, and the next day it was 'Raquel', a new version of the name, which we followed keenly. Hearing of a fall, my stomach lurched, but no, she was soon up and kicking on. Once or twice falls had resulted in a night in hospital, but luckily this didn't happen in Holland, and we rushed to the finish to hear all about the round and how horse and rider had coped.

Show jumping, which came the following day, was a worry too. We watched, willing the poles to stay in place, Jack in his enthusiasm often lifting his leg subconsciously as our rider took each fence. We have noticed other parents doing this at local shows.

I think Rachel and Chips ended up in fifteenth place out of sixty-three, after the fall on the cross country, but she was presented with a bouquet and a plaque. Yes, even the men received flowers which seemed a strange custom to us.

On the last evening there was a great get together where everyone could relax with the tension over, and we joined in the dancing which followed the meal. On our last morning we did souvenir shopping, especially for real clogs for the family. We had difficulty in finding them and with the language, too, as we had to go to a farm warehouse. The drive back was rather worrying as we feared we might miss the ferry.

We hadn't even taken a camera on this trip, but it was an era of colour slides, and many of our friends were enthusiasts in this line. It became the thing to show slides when entertaining. Holidays abroad were shown with running commentaries, and I honestly enjoyed them, and learned a lot about other countries. Jack, however, was inclined to doze off in the warmth, comfort and darkness.

Farming methods were still changing throughout this decade. We employed less labour and the cottage in the village was given up. We were still sharing labour and machinery with the Stringers, and this method was working well. We kept a Jersey cow, and I made a little butter in a glass churn. Jack enjoyed the thick cream with his fruit pies which were still his favourite puddings. Prices recorded were "ten gimmers bought — £11.5s. and three calves — £19 each."

In the kitchen there was a new Jackson cooker with an eye-level grill and a warming drawer, which I found very useful. There was a small second-hand fridge in the dairy. Although the dairy faced north and was cool most of the year, it was a treat to be able to keep lettuce crisp, cream from going sour, and meat from having to be cooked twice.

A pretty Axminster carpet with floral design covered the sitting room floor 'wall to wall'! This was a great joy and looked so luxurious I had to keep going to the doorway for the pleasure of just looking at it.

CHAPTER 20

The 1970's started off with Tony's marriage to Pam Bell on a cold January day in North Cave church. There was a very good and happy reception at Cave Castle, which I hadn't seen since dancing displays on the lawn at garden parties in the Tommy Foster days, and in the evening guests came to Cot Nab to round off the celebrations.

Austin Bell provided music for dancing with his electric organ, which had been brought in the previous evening, and once more the kitchen table was taken outside and the fun continued into the small hours of the morning.

We were delighted to welcome Pam into the family. She was not only another secretary to take care of accounts (the brown paper parcels had long since been replaced by a more efficient system), but was an extra good tractor driver too. As her mother, Grace, died the following year, we hoped she looked on us all as her family too.

The Estate provided Tony and Pam with a small cottage in the hamlet of Uncleby, a few miles away, a name which had intrigued us in our early days on the Wolds. It was just a straggle of farmhouses and cottages which hid in a fold of the hills with a Methodist chapel which had sadly become redundant. This chapel was later converted as a store place for Tony's collection of vintage tractors, and I thought of the happy Anniversaries and other special services in this remote little chapel, while regretting the sad change. The first time we discovered Uncleby we had been amazed to find the lanes filled with parked cars. "Gracious," we said, "Whatever is going on here?" only to discover later it had been the Chapel Anniversary.

Before the days of motor vehicles, families would walk miles to the Chapel, and some, perhaps, would go by pony traps. The lanes were then gated to prevent stock straying, and the posts are still to be seen on the roadside. The hill was difficult in snow, being the sort which drifted in, but Tony, in the years he travelled to and fro, was never quite defeated, though he came near to it in the worst winters.

By this time we had a large deep freeze in the storeroom and Tony also got one, so we didn't have the worry of getting bread and other perishable foods when snowed up. The butcher announced one day that he could no longer continue his round of wold farms except for occasional deliveries in bulk. So, that was that! I had been saying for years "I don't need a freezer, we have nothing to put in it. We don't grow our own fruit or veg, what use would it be?" The vegetable garden had become part of the enlarged yard some years earlier. Well, I soon found out that I couldn't do without the invaluable deep freeze. Apart from the meat and bread, I stocked it with pies and cakes. We went in summer to 'pick your own' fruit farms, we bought fish and chickens in bulk, and suddenly the whole pattern of shopping and catering changed for the better. Why had I waited so long to join the enthusiastic users of deep freeze techniques?

I had continued with large baking days, but now I could have a good session and freeze half of it. This was especially useful when planning to feed visitors. If we were given pheasants, neither Jack nor Tony were keen on shooting, I froze the odd brace, and this caused some amusement when I decided to take such a brace to our friends Jim and Mary, when we visited them in their retirement home in Wales. I put the bag containing the pheasants near the top of the freezer so that I could find it easily as we were leaving for the car journey. In the last minute rush I grabbed the bag and wrapped it in lots of newspaper. On arrival I presented Mary with the package saying, "For the freezer. You'll enjoy them when we have gone home!"

Some time after this little holiday I received a letter thanking me for the strawberries. I couldn't help laughing, but I was better off for pheasants than strawberries which I was quite sorry to lose. I had packed them in little plastic cartons as I find that they go less mushy in this way, but when quickly rolling the newspapers around the package, I hadn't noticed the knobbly shapes.

Growing peas for 'Birds Eye' had become commonplace by this time. Though we never went in for this crop, we luckily had neighbours who did. When the vining machines had departed from the fields, after sometimes working throughout the night, we rushed in, like gleaners of old, to gather armfuls of what was left on the headlands or on an awkward hill end. Filling the back of the Landrover with the vines, we would come home to pull off the pods then to shell and blanche them to get dozens of little bagfuls into the freezer, post haste. The quicker the better, we were told, and we knew that 'Birds Eye' ensured that the peas were vined when just right and had to be rushed to the factories with little delay. It was often late at night when our little freezing operations were finished.

For special occasions and at Christmas time I could now plan ahead, and put every sort of savoury or sweet dish safely away till needed. It became not so much what to cook as what to unfreeze.

The older members of my family, two sisters Lallie and Olive, and step-sister Dorothy, always came at Christmas as they lived alone. Lallie and Dorothy, with advancing age and infirmity, needed quite a lot of looking after as well as Lill. Some years the visits were staggered, as both Lallie and Dorothy had long train journeys and liked to stay for two weeks, longer in the summer, but overlapped for Christmas week. Olive, who lived nearer, would come for only a few days.

It was fortunate that we had the spare rooms and our family living near didn't need beds. They were all good about inviting us to a festive meal, but I did a lot of entertaining too. The freezer, plus long lists of daily menus, helped at such times. I also had a large Moffat cooker which we bought in an auction sale and it was a boon for large baking sessions.

After the holiday, I had a few anxious moments getting the elderly and infirm sisters to their respective trains. Whoever drove us to York station left me to actually go on to the platform as there were barriers still, and the chauffeur probably had other urgent business to see to on the way back to the farm. Dorothy had to be taken under the line, and even if we were lucky enough to get a porter, it wasn't all that easy. The trains had such a short stop, and once I nearly got carried off too, when taking baggage into the carriage.

Another time I pushed Lallie in quickly, saw to her suitcase, waved through the window and then realised I was still holding her hand luggage including a packet of sandwiches. I opened the train door just before it moved, and threw in the bag saying, "Please pass that to the little old lady in the red coat in the right hand carriage!"

The most worrying time was when I, for some reason, had to cope with both of them alone. I think I had decided to stay in York and shop as I sometimes did when the bus still ran past the farm gate. There was half an hour between the London and Bristol trains, so I saw Dorothy settled on a seat and told her not to move till I came back. Then I took Lallie to the Kings Cross train, thinking how very frail and vacant she looked, and hoped there would be no delay with a taxi meeting her on the platform in London. Back to Dorothy, down the lift, under the line, quite a walk, and then up again in time for her train. The gap between that platform and the train step was extra wide, and with Dorothy needing to hold her walking stick, I had to literally push her up by her ample buttocks! We were very pleased to be able to have them all to stay with us, and they were so grateful, but by the time I had done the station stint, I felt quite drained and exhausted.

Soon after the New Year I would start my mad spring cleaning sessions, but felt it was necessary as I skimped on housework during the year, and after Lill became ill I had a period of not having any help in the house.

The kitchen floor had new Vinolay, in a Roman-tile pattern which made cleaning much easier, and Jack covered the dairy floor with a cheap lino so now there were only red quarry tiles in the store room and back passage. They didn't get scrubbed very often either! Now, of course, they are much sought after for "olde world" effect.

The garden took up quite a lot of time, especially coping with large areas of herbaceous borders which, over the years, kept getting out of hand and assumed a jungle-like appearance between thinning out or cutting down sessions. The weeds crept in from the hedge bottoms and the rockery became overgrown at times, but the tarmac drive

Jack with his sheep and "Glen".

85

was much easier than the ever weed-ridden gravel, thought it didn't look so nice.

We abandoned the tennis court as such when the wire needed replacing and the family were no longer at home. It made a good space for the grandchildren to play on, or, with sheep netting set round, it could be grazed by Jack's ewes and their lambs.

Jack had reluctantly sold the sheep, other than the Jacobs, when he found the work was becoming too hard, especially the setting of nets in winter. Tony's interests lay mainly in arable farming rather than in stock rearing, but after the sheep had gone a suckler herd was started with forty three-month-old Angus Friesian calves. These were in time served by a seven-eighths Charolais bull, and calved at two years and three months.

The offspring being fattened and finished at two years, it was a pleasing sight to watch the cows with calves in the dale in summer, or in the large fold yard in winter, deep in clean straw.

CHAPTER 21

The grandchildren were now a very lively addition to our family circle, as all eight were near enough to be frequent visitors, especially when Maureen's three little girls lived next door.

In some ways they seemcd like one large family as they played in house or garden. When the parents went out for an evening they never needed sitters-in as all the children, if necessary could spend the night with us to be collected the next morning. So they came, at various stages, from carrycots to proper beds.

On rare occasions all eight were left in our charge, once for a whole weekend when it was rather chaotic, especially as two were recovering from chickenpox. One afternoon, when a bit of squabbling had been going on, I took Michelle to the kitchen and had a game of ping pong on the large table!

But how much easier this generation of little ones were compared with ours when young. The simple clothes, for one thing — Babygrows, all-in-one garments for outdoors, near non-iron fabrics, and the joy of automatic washing machines. I especially appreciated the wonderful little "Baby-relax" chairs to prop up the babies when bored with lying flat. Strapped in safely and set up on the big table well out of draughts, the baby was able to have a good view of all that was going on. Bathing was done in the bathroom rather than in front of the fire, changing took place on a special mat, never on one's knee and, joy of joys, plastic pants which save so much washing, and potty training for tinies became less important.

Luckily our family all believed in a certain amount of discipline for their childrten, and on the whole they were well behaved and easy to look after. Their Mums weren't the types who over-reacted to parenthood and never devoted all the day to either fussing over or educating their offspring practically from birth.

The last two of this batch — Sarah (Maureen's) and Mark (Pam's) — were only a few months apart in age and got on extremely well together. Mark, being the first grandson, took on the traditional Dewbury as his second name for first sons of first sons, a tradition which had continued in the Megginson family for generations.

When Mark and Sarah were still under school age, I looked after

Grand-children in the garden.

them for most of the day while their mothers were helping with taties. By then, of course, the hand pickers had gone and, in spite of people saying Wold land was too stony for such machines as we had bought, they worked well. There weren't many for 'looance, about half a dozen altogether, but I was quite busy all the time. I had a help with brass polishing and floor washing again, one day a week, but that help stopped as Doris was one of the gang on the machine!

Tony, Pam, Maureen and the children had their midday meal with us and I always preferred to dish up a hot dinner at noon. One afternoon, after a harassing day, the two little ones were getting to a rare squabbling stage. I remember desperately rushing to the toy cupboard to find a change of game to distract them saying angrily, "I'm absolutely sick of you two. You'll drive me up the bloody wall!" A stunned silence followed, and I quickly changed my tune, hoping the swear word would be forgotten. It was, until weeks later when Mark said to his Daddy, "Do you know what Grannie said to me and Sarah?" — and so it all came out!

During the times when my elderly and somewhat handicapped

sisters visited us, and the children were around too, I began to think I would qualify for a job in either a geriatric ward or a nursery school. Sometimes there were emergency calls from a harassed parent, and one morning after Sally had started school, Jennifer telephoned to say that Redecca, aged three, had just drunk half a bottle of cough mixture. The doctor had advised that she should be taken to hospital quickly and kept awake. Derek was working away and I was asked if I could help. I stopped whatever job was in hand, left a message for Jack and was ready when Jennifer drove into the yard. I shall always remember that drive to York, trying to keep Rebecca awake while worrying if she would be all right. Then, as before, when Maureen was in hospital, I left Jennifer with her daughter to have her tummy washed out and returned on the mid-day bus. Luckily Rebecca soon recovered, but it was alarming at the time.

All eight children, as they reached primary school age, went to Bugthorpe C of E school, and we all felt it a wonderfully happy place with good, yet fairly strict staff who made lessons really interesting. While there, at the age of nine, Rebecca wrote a very vivid poem about the Vikings which I have kept and still feel proud of this inspired effort. I attended all the usual functions and Jack joined me for the Christmas concert when, like all grandparents, we were proud of the children taking part. One year all eight were there together.

This new type of education was so imaginative and I found much to interest me in the exhibitions set up for special projects. Jack and I were asked to give a talk one afternoon on 'The way we used to live' and were pleasantly surprised by the interest shown. Recalling my youth and a way of life long gone, helped to set me off on the idea of writing it all down. The boys were keen to hear Jack's version of farming life before tractors were in general use and asked many questions. We little thought that the hard times we had experienced would be worth recording.

Only three of the grandchildren have inherited our great love of horses, but perhaps that is enough with the ever-increasing costs of everything connected with the world of horses, especially at competition level. I have often thought of the household things and worldly goods we could have purchased with the money we chose to use on our horsey activities, but the pleasure we enjoyed together in this way was well worth any sacrifice.

The equestrian sports have become so much more professional

than in the days of our family involvement. Competition is very keen and it would be unusual for a girl to make her way up to a high level on the shoestring method which Rachel used. All tack and clothing, plus the expense of getting round the country with a horse, to say nothing of escalating entry fees, has limited such activities. In fact, there are so many entries for horse trials that they are accepted on a ballot system, and riders are lucky to get in at all in the areas they choose.

However, it is fortunate that the grand-daughters are happy to ride for the love of it, although we did have a short period of being Pony Club supporters second time round, and Jennifer became a kitchen helper in camp week.

Our dressing up box was a constant delight to the children. It was an old farm lad's box and stood on the landing where there was plenty of space to play. It held old fancy dress costumes, a large variety of hats, my pre-war black velvet cape and a miscellaneous assortment of cast off outdated garments. High-heeled shoes were popular, especially the silver or gold dancing variety. The little girls would go teetering down the stairs and often round the garden, walking with difficulty in high-heeled sandals several sizes too big.

One March day, when Mothering Sunday coincided with my birthday, we had a large lunch party with all the family. It was usual for some of them to come for Sunday lunch, but this was a special celebration. I cooked large dishes of giant-sized shepherds' pie and a casserole with lots of vegetables. The family turned up with a wonderful variety of puddings. By setting up a gate-legged table at one end of the kitchen, as well as the normal one, it was rather a squash to move around, but all were seated. I see from an old photograph of this occasion that Auntie Lallie was with us, and some of the children were wearing dressing-up clothes.

We had kept a lot of our childrens' games and books, at least all the favourite ones, and these all came out again, including my old draughts board/cum ludo/cum horse racing game. This, in a large box, was one of my Christmas presents when about ten years old. It was labelled, in the fashion of that time, 'A compendium of games'. Things were well made then, and it is still in the toy drawer and hasn't even split in the folds. I still treasure my favourite books and pre-war annuals which amuse the present day children, and may be worth a fortune some day.

Jack's old horse-on-wheels called Jess is still with us though

Feeding the family in the kitchen. Note the children's table in the background.

looking the worse for wear as he is over seventy years old. Originally a very splendid animal covered with real pony skin and wearing a very grand saddle and bridle, he has suffered from generations of the little ones' love for him.

I have always enjoyed making clothes for dolls and teddies, though my stitching leaves much to be desired. With the new generation I was frequently asked to make things. The up-to-date walkie-talkie dolls needed a lot of material for their dresses, but I could usually find some old garment to cut up for this job. Jane's portly Paddington needed pyjamas, as did Sarah's Big Ted and only recently Sarah was looking at an old photograph of me and exclaimed, "You were wearing the dress which you made into Big Ted's pyjamas!" I never liked to waste anything, a throwback to the war years of make do and mend. To this day, I get more satisfaction from making draught excluder dogs from old fabric coats from Oxfam, or jumble sales, than in using new material.

CHAPTER 22

Another wedding took place in January 1974 when Rachel married Norman Webb. Like Tony, he chose January as one of the slacker months of the farming year. Not many months leave enough spare time for a wedding and honeymoon, however brief the latter might be.

The previous November, Rachel and many eventing friends had been thrilled to attend a reception and the wedding service of Princess Anne and Mark Phillips. The present sent off from Rachel was an Acorn stool, with suitable carvings. Mr. Granger of Acorn Industries had been delighted to carry out this commission.

Rachel had so many horsey friends, up and down the country as well as those near home, that we sent out some two hundred invitations, thinking that a lot of the far-flung guests would never risk coming, especially to the Yorkshire Wolds in mid winter, with some talk at that time of petrol rationing. As it happened, the weather was comparatively mild, and those who drove from Scotland or Cornwall, to mention extremes, all reached us without difficulty. Bed and breakfast offers had come in from local friends as well as family.

We had a house full of guests for afternoon tea when the great day of Rachel's wedding arrived, as the service was an evening one at 5.30 p.m. This was the era of long dresses for women on all evening occasions. We even wore them to supper with friends, or to the theatre and the young children also got all 'dolled up' for their parties in angle length frocks, and very sweet they looked too. So, for the evening wedding, most ladies wore long gowns and luckily the church was warm. I had had the long coat of my matching two-piece outfit specially lined in case I felt frozen.

We decorated the pew ends with Christmas roses and greenery entwined with horse shoes, laboriously painted silver, and hung on white ribbons. The church was especially lovely at night and the colours of the lighted windows shone out to give a welcome sight as guests walked up the path.

We were proud of the four little grand-daughter bridesmaids, two in tartan taffeta and two smaller ones in white with red sashes. I am

92

sure their mothers breathed sighs of relief when they all behaved well.

After a very late meal at the Corn Mill at Stamford Bridge, many people came back to the house to see the presents and to drink coffee. We also entertained fifteen to lunch the following day, once more putting an extra table in the kitchen. Much work and advance planning goes into such family occasions, but it is all worthwhile to have happy memories.

As usual we were in a last minute rush to get changed. The bride had friends to help her, but we struggled into our finery with little time to spare. Jack, like the bridegroom, wore his evening suit of the white tie and tails variety, and it wasn't till we looked at photographs later that we realised he had never worn the white waistcoat. My fault, of course, for not putting it out on the bed! I went bare-headed to church, having attempted to make a little hat to match my ensemble. I tried it on to laughter from all. Lucy said, "Grannie you look like a monkey!" so it was never worn.

CHAPTER 23

When we knew Rachel was going to be married, and would naturally take her horse with her to her new farm home, Jack decided it would be a nice change to have a rest from horses for a bit. But this idea was short lived. Seeing an advertisement in 'Horse and Hound' stating that two unbroken, well-matched Welsh ponies were for sale, he had to telephone and arrange to see them with the idea of driving them.

We went off early one morning heading for Mold in Wales, with the trailer behind the Landrover. Jack liked the look of the ponies, loaded them up and off we went again, heading for home.

So started the Tom and Jerry era. Jack really enjoyed breaking in these little identical grey ponies, and making use of his driving skills again after so many years. Slowly he brought them on with much lungeing, long-reining and eventually getting them to pull a log of wood. He drove them daily, either singly or as a pair, using the wide grass verge to get them used to heavy traffic. Later he walked miles

Jack driving "Tom" and "Jerry".

behind them, sometimes standing on the heavy log. Eventually he bought a rulley, a Yorkshire term for a flat cart or trolley with iron tyres and then came the great day of yoking them up.

This took place in a cultivated field for safety. He knew from past experience with cart horses that being too hurried, or taking short cuts when dealing with young ponies, could have disastrous results and ruin their trust and confidence for life. However, all went according to plan. The little chaps took the strain of the rulley and, pulling to the manor born, set off on a drive round the lanes.

Annie, a friend of Rachel's from Devon, had offered to stay on after the wedding and to work for us. She especially wanted to help Jack in lambing time. This was towards the end of keeping a flock of ewes and Annie also loved helping with the pony driving, keeping Jack company on many a freezingly cold drive. Once he started driving the pair, he did so daily until he felt they were really safe and reliable.

I, too, enjoyed driving in all sorts of weathers, well wrapped up, but usually returned almost stiff with cold. The iron wheels rattled along the roads as we went along at a good fast trot. The hills proved no problem, and the game little chaps pulled well going up and learned to hold back going down. Hill work develops muscles and Tom and Jerry became very fit indeed.

It wasn't long before a four wheel Ralli car was bought at a Reading sale. This particular style of vehicle was called after a man called Ralli, and was similar to a dogcart and had two seats back to back. Jack enjoyed entering a few classes at local shows as the ponies and cart could all go in the Ivor Williams trailer.

We enjoyed taking part in the Walkington Hayride, which involved dressing up in Victorian costume. I was loaned a genuine poke bonnet and other items of clothing. Owing to the steady pace of the heavy horses which led the procession through villages around the Beverley area, it was a long day's drive and our ponies were frustrated at being held back to keep in line. However it was all good fun and the collecting boxes carried by enthusiasts on foot raised a lot of money for various charities.

Jack was later persuaded to enter driving competitions under F.E.I. rules, and we set off to compete at Lowther Castle in Cumbria, not really knowing what we had let ourselves in for. It was worse, in some ways, than being involved in horse trials or show jumping, with the double harness — two sets, one for 'best' — and

95

"Tom" and "Jerry" with Ralli-car and family.

the vehicle to keep clean, too. We arrived at the tented stables in front of the ruined castle and found which were our three allocated boxes all in a row, one for each pony, and one for us to turn into a bed-sitting room!

Hotels were not even considered, so we took camp beds, sleeping bags, a little cooking stove and a supply of food, and I made our quarters as comfy as possible while Jack saw to the ponies. Then followed the course inspection with cars or Landrovers to take us round after the initial briefing.

We didn't sleep too well in our loose box with horses or ponies behind us and on either side. We never quite realised before what an almost continuous succession of noises they make during the night, munching, snorting, heavy breathing, to say nothing of peeing and farting!

The weather was very hot, and temperature in the eighties. Jack had to recap on his dressage test and to remember and work out the best way to drive through the hazards. Hazards, which are part of the marathon, are obstacles to be negotiated in a set time with numerous tricky twists and turns between trees or man-made fencing. The river crossing at Lowther was quite wide and deep for small ponies.

Lowther Park is one of the most beautiful places I have seen, but

96

the areas around the decayed castle are sad to look at. We walked under the ancient yews, planted for bows and arrows, and round the little pathways which, like the ornamental pools, were overgrown. These had once been picturesque walks for Lord Lonsdale, the Yellow Earl, and his many house guests in the heyday of the Earl's extravagant way of life. Having read the biography of this famous aristocrat, I was especially interested to be in the vicinity of the castle, built in a period of prosperity; yet with unbelievable speed the great fortunes were spent and the decline of the Lowthers began. The present earl lives in a more modest house, but the colours of the family livery are still to be seen on the yellow estate vehicles.

We found our fellow competitors and grooms were very friendly and helpful to us, such novices, in this sport. We chatted with the top 'whips' and heard interesting stories of their lives and their horses.

The dressage test was Jack's least favourite part of the competition, but he managed to remember the various movements. I had to wear a jockey cap, jodphurs and black jacket, borrowed from the family, and my ancient black leather hunting boots in order to look like a well turned out groom. I sat very still on the rear seat of the vehicle, back to back with the driver, and yet had to be ready to jump down quickly if necessary to hold the ponies' heads.

The heat of the day increased before we set off on the seventeen mile marathon, but we could wear cool clothes. We had to carry a referee to make sure we kept to the course, and to record scores. The lady allocated to us proved to be the wife of Lord Lonsdale's agent, and Jack enjoyed the conversation on the long seventeen mile drive. Since then, the small pony pairs no longer carry referees.

Jack made no effort to go fast as there had been warnings about dehydration in the heat, so he didn't want to overdo Tom and Jerry. The parkland was beautiful and there were compulsory stops for veterinary inspection. Our gallant little ponies did their best, but we lost marks when Jack let them resort to a walk when most of the course had to be done at a trot. The hazards presented little problems as Jack had the skill necessary to drive through the tricky places, and the ponies responded without mistakes being made. I often took up a kneeling position on my back seat, partly to cling on and partly to see where we were going by facing forward. I got a lot of bruises on my legs as much of the course was rough and bumpy. We crossed the river without difficulty, encouraged by the cheers of spectators on either bank.

After the long drive we reached the finish and trotted into the main arena. The commentator gave our dreadful number of time faults, while congratulating Jack on completing his first marathon.

Washing down ponies and vehicle took up some time, and we were helped by the more professional types with horses and other equipment. I have seldom felt more sweaty and dirty and resorted to filling a bucket with warm water and, after carrying it to the privacy of the trailer, having a stand up wash down while standing in the bucket! The Duke of Edinburgh was competing with his four-in-hand and seemed to thoroughly enjoy it all, but I think he would have better bathing facilities!

We felt very proud to join in the parade, after doing the final competition of cone driving, and we took our places in the long lines of every type of horse and vehicle, from teams of Cleveland bays to tiny but courageous Shetland ponies. We were presented with our rosette and enjoyed trotting round the arena in the blazing sunshine.

I had written an article on the training of Tom and Jerry for the 'Light Horse' magazine and did some reviews of driving books, so I felt quite pleased to be asked to cover Lowther and send in my report. A journalist indeed!

The aftermath from such a trip was even worse than after other horsey activities — all that unpacking, cleaning and putting away — but we weren't deterred and returned the following and successive years. Cirencester Park was another venue and there we had first class accommodation for ourselves and ponies with the Tucker family from Tetbury. Other horsey friends, the Raymonds from Devon, joined us in Cirencester Park on the marathon day, as did Ellis, Margery and Anne from Wiltshire, so it was a lovely reunion.

We also competed at Tatton Park, Cheshire, near our old friends Betty and Tom, who found it strange that we should occupy ourselves so much with Tom and Jerry that we had no time to walk round the famous gardens. Tom and Jerry had to go into stables a few miles from Tatton Park, so we had quite a lot of journeys to and fro our friends' house where we breakfasted and sneaked out quietly in the early mornings.

Another time we took Tony's precious caravan. I say 'precious' because, like anything else belonging to our son, it had to be carefully looked after. We also took the Landrover and trailer to trials at Beamish and Nostell Priory. Our old friend Joan took her car to tow the caravan and was a great help as second groom.

I was fortunate in being able to be away from home, where Maureen was in charge of dogs, 'looances, and looking after poor Lill. The second time we went to Lowther, harvest operations were in full swing, so Jack decided he could only spare one night away from home. The ponies' boxes were already booked and because we had been accepted as competitors, we had not only the special badges but also an invitation to a party on Derwent Island with Mr. and Mrs. Managed as hosts.

We thoroughly enjoyed being relaxed spectators on the marathon day, and afterwards changed in our stable, emerging in full evening dress which did seem somewhat incongruous. We drove to Keswick where the police were supervising parking and then walked along the shore of Derwent Water, feeling rather self-conscious before the crowd of interested holidaymakers. Showing our special passes we walked down the landing stage to our boat with a ferryman waiting to take us across to the brightly lit island.

I had always been fascinated by islands, and that evening seemed full of magic. Because Prince Philip was also a guest, this was truly a royal occasion. We joined other competitors, officials and many more guests for drinks in the lovely home before adjourning to a large marquee on the lawn for supper and dancing. Very sensibly we were offered a substantial casserole dish with delicious puff pastry pieces. All the guests would have had only picnic meals during the day, so were ready to tuck in to the good hot food, followed by delicious sweets. After joining in the dancing for an hour or two, we had a moonlit boat ride back to the lake shore. It was a wonderful memory of Lowther, even if the ponies stayed behind.

After a few years, Jack began to think this F.E.I. sport was too much of a 'hallock', and decided to revert to just driving for fun and later on became involved with Driving for the Disabled.

He disliked the long road journeys with the trailer, but I have always felt that had he been a wealthy man, and able to employ a chauffeur and groom, preferably young, and to buy the best type of fast moving ponies, he would still be competing!

CHAPTER 24

Our church life became more busy as time went on. We had been on the Council for many years, but now Jack was a Churchwarden and I the Secretary. When Rachel heard this announcement she remarked, "Oh dear, Mum's Minutes will be hours!" One gets the truth from families, and they often cut one down to size, which is not a bad thing.

We are fortunate to have such a beautiful church in which to worship. St. Edith's dates from Norman times and was restored by Sir Tatton Sykes in the middle of the last century. The roof is of a colourful painted design with gold leaf decoration and the very unusual floor of marble mosaic with a pattern of exotic birds is copied from a similar floor in the Vatican.

One vicar was surprised on entering the church to discover two people crawling towards each other across the floor calling out, "Here's another", or "I've found another sort". They were trying to find how many varieties of birds were included in the floor design.

While the church is a place of great beauty, it is too large from a practical point of view. The cost of maintaining the fabric and keeping the building warm enough for winter services is very high, but we struggle on, as do many other small parishes. There is much brass, too much as seen from the cleaners' point of view. However, our little band of volunteers, mostly elderly, do their best for the love of St. Edith's.

As a complete contrast, Givendale church, a few miles away, is so small and simple. It stands in a very peaceful situation, tucked away from the road in a clump of trees. The views down the dale include ponds and grassy banks which in spring are covered with snowdrops and aconites. I love that little church on Harvest Festival evenings when, in the soft light of candles, it takes on an old world glow, though I must admit it is sometimes difficult to make out the words of the hymns.

Lord Irwin, later the second Earl of Halifax, who then lived in the hamlet of Great Givendale, used to read a lesson and I recall him borrowing Cecil Jackson's glasses and saying later, "Those are fine Cecil. I must get a pair like them!"

Our Harvest Festivals on Thursday evenings have sometimes been followed by a special supper in the village hall, but I often invited people back to Cot Nab for a simple soup and apple pie meal. I don't think the food need be elaborate, it's the getting together and friendship that really matters. I feel that about all entertaining, though I do try to give food which my guests will enjoy. Looking back, I wonder how I coped with all the visitors, callers for meals and weekend guests, especially when kitchen equipment was somewhat primitive. My efforts can't have been too bad though as they kept returning.

We always had two or three fund raising events for the church during the year, but in the late 'seventies we had an especially enthusiastic vicar plus a big Appeal Fund, so various extra activities were organised.

One winter night, luckily there was no snow, we opened our house for a Games Evening, as something different. We tried to cater for all ages, so Maureen had the young ones in her house and we arranged every sort of indoor game in both rooms, hall and landing. I wonder now how we heated it all? We must have borrowed extra portable fires I think. Supper was in the kitchen, and a film show was in a bedroom. The film was on driving activities, and I can still see the disappointment on the faces of some children who came up having heard the words 'Tom and Jerry'. They expected cartoons!

However, it all went well, with a hundred people milling around or sitting quietly absorbed at a card table. One group went on so long, perhaps playing Monopoly, that we thought they would stay all night.

On Rogation Sunday, for three years, we had a service in our yard near the potato store where we could retreat if wet, and that was really most impressive. All the choir, and there were some keen youngsters at that time, wore their robes and sang in procession round the field behind the vicar and wardens who were carrying their staffs. Afterwards they came to the kitchen for tea and buns and ate them in the garden, though one time it was so cold that we found room for around thirty in the house.

The barn dances for the church and Save the Children funds took place for several years in mid-June. By then we had a very large potato store in two sections, all insulated with air ducts in one half. Getting ready was an upheaval and much hard work. All pallets were moved and piled up to make tables in the supper department.

101

Before we used the pallet system, straw bales were used as seating, with old rugs, or curtains, spread over to stop the prickles and trestle tables had to be hired. Pallets were easier all round and people could sit on them in groups.

The largest trailer was placed at one end as a platform for the band, with kitchen chairs for seating. But the first, and worst, job was the clearing out and sweeping up. That made clouds of dust so one could hardly see across the store. Fortunately a gang from Save the Children came up from Pocklington to help as well as the Bishop Wilton folk. Then came the more interesting part, the decorating which was left till the evening before the dance as we used a lot of fresh greenery and, again, paper flowers with the addition of strings of flags and balloons. The old tennis net made a good foundation when stretched along a wall and it had greenery threaded through it.

We worried about the loo problem, and one year hired little cabin-like cubicles. Later, we put notices for the Ladies to go to the house, quite a long trot, and Gents near a door at the back of the building with a second notice outside reading "Anywhere between here and Brid!" The wood did make a screen from the road.

Supper was made, or collected up, by all the working party, and we always had plenty, and a good variety of refreshments set out on individual plates. We hired boilers for the tea and provided large jugs of orange squash "to sleck dust". Mrs. Mitchell was the "caller" and brought her band, and a really great time was had by all. It was amazing that as many as three hundred came, yet it never got out of hand as Kathy Mitchell had the knack of keeping order in the nicest way. Even people who knew nothing of country dancing joined in and others helped to sort them out or point them in the right direction. The grandchildren, with young friends, were full of enthusiasm once they got over their initial shyness.

It was always a hectic weekend for us in all ways, and some years it coincided with the Kirby Underdale garden party, another important local function. I hated to miss this afternoon in the Rectory garden, always blessed with sunshine, with family involved and the children in fancy dress. It was a really old fashioned affair, with teas served on the lawn, looking down on the squat tower of the old church, visible below the flight of stone steps, with the rolling hills as a background.

So I usually went for a couple of hours, plus getting ready for weekend guests who always asked, "When's the Barn Dance and can we come?" Once, eight of them crossed the Pennines for this occasion, and were fitted in somewhere to sleep. Luckily they didn't mind being allocated jobs, whether it was amusing children, cutting sandwiches or putting food on dozens of plates!

Mary did mind one year, when the Jacob ram, who was penned up for a "Guess His Weight" competition, jumped out and scared her. With his extra long horns, I must admit he did look dangerous. It was safe other years to lead a pony round in the interval for a similar guessing game whch raised money, as well as the raffle, and folk liked to see the animals.

In 1978, Lord Halifax's racehorse, Shirley Heights, won the Derby, the greatest honour in the world of flat racing and the ambition of every owner. So, later on, a big party and champagne reception was held at Garrowby in the early evening and once more a marquee appeared in the park. Unfortunately it was the same evening as our Barn Dance, but we couldn't miss that occasion. So, off we went, Jack and I, leaving last minute jobs to our family and guests. We got back in time for the first dance and the champagne didn't even make us dizzy.

It was always very late when the last of our close friends, neighbours and the band left the kitchen, after drinking coffee and eating leftovers from the supper, but we really enjoyed those happy dances in the tatie store.

The worst part, other than Tony's efforts in cleaning the place beforehand, was the clearing up afterwards. Helpers came on the Monday evening, but it made a lot of work for Tony with such a disruption in that part of the farm.

CHAPTER 25

The pattern of farming was gradually changing and when the Stringers acquired more land, our partnership in sharing implements and labour, came to an end. It had been a very satisfactory venture which helped both families.

Now, however, we needed a corndrier for ourselves so another building was adapted. The Dutch barn became part of the drying set up, with simplex bins, catwalks, grain pit and a fan, the latter driven by an old combine engine. This complicated, or so it seemed to me, factory-like complex took months to complete, but it proved a good system which has lasted well.

Our townee friends marvelled at all this and were taken for a tour, with the braver ones trying the catwalk. Some of them wondered about the capital outlay involved. So did I.

Every year had its ups and downs. There were heatwave summers, with the worry of the barley dying off, and in 1976 all combining was finished with the straw cleared up by August 20th. Yet again, one year we had snow at Easter. Tractors became more powerful with quiet, air-conditioned cabs, and drivers listened to the radio or cassettes as they drove over the land. We had come a long way from the whistling plough lads. No longer was it necessary to wrap up well for tractor work, and there was little use for the piled up, thick old overcoats which still lived under the back stairs. Some weighed heavily and became even more so when sopping wet. Drying them in front of the fire used to be a bad weather ritual. The aroma is remembered as I write — pungent is the word!

A super-flo, triple K, and rotovator were recent acquisitions in the implement line, with a four furrow reversible plough, and the new cock-pheasant, and bale carrier for haytime. So much machinery to maintain. Tony now had a well stocked workshop at one end of the big shed, with an inspection pit. The layout of the farm buildings had changed considerably since the 'fifties, as larger and more valuable implements took up extra storage space.

The old granary became a chitting store, as it was now considered necessary for the spuds to be sprouted before planting, helped by controlled lighting. The changeover to the pallet method advocated

104

a forklift truck. These "progressive" years seemed one long outlay to keep up with it all.

The potato harvester made one of the greatest changes, as the whole process was updated with gradual improvements and the workers were now protected from the elements. It did, however, still involve family labour plus other "casuals".

I have already described the effect of coping with the little ones while Maureeen and Pam worked in tatie-time, Maureen on the harvester and Pam driving the tractor and trailer to and from the store. To keep the operations going as long as possible, an evening shift was organised, so Jack and I took a turn on this while Maureen took over Pam's children as well as her own, from 4.30 to 7.00 p.m. We sometimes wondered which job was best, as teas for the children were often difficult with some not liking the proposed menu. The ones returning from school could be tired and cross, too.

For a short period, Tony had the bright idea of an early morning shift as well, and I staggered out on this session. I remember how cold one's fingers were, and the relief I felt when I could dash back to the kitchen fire for breakfast. Luckily, this shift system didn't last.

Of course there were wet days, some years far too many of them, when from the women's point of view, they were an opportunity to catch up on neglected housework. I still think the cultivation of seed potatoes is the most harassing of all crops, and when prices are low it can be soul destroying.

Combining went on at harvest time till the small hours of the night if the weather was right, but the workforce was small compared with earlier times of harvesting. I sent out flasks of soup and sandwiches on late night sessions, but on the whole the men still liked their apple pie, which they got most mornings throughout the year, fruit bread, and other pastries. We had several large flasks for the tea which were so much easier than the old way of having to make the drinks just before they were needed.

Being so close to the busy road, the combine had to be equipped with numerous lights. It made quite a show as it came clattering along and into the yard. The old Massey 500 hadn't a cab, and Tony, the driver, got very dirty and dusty. Packed dinners were eaten in the field with someone taking over the wheel to keep the machine going non-stop.

It was late to bed on fine harvest nights, waiting to give Jack and Tony a hot meal, though by the 'seventies, Pam provided that for

Tony. Jack was usually on the "straw" side and finished work earlier.

The hoes were no longer used, as a few swedes were sown "broadcast", and corn and potato crops sprayed. The last time Jack used the old fiddle-drill, he had an easy job, sitting on the bonnet of the Landrover being driven slowly round the field.

The last years of shepherding became easier with the use of electric nets, but Jack felt that the sheep must go if Tony wasn't interested in keeping them. We were sorry to finish with sheep, other than a few Jacobs, as they had been part of our lives ever since Jack and I first met in my school holidays. The Jacob lambs were very pretty and the tup so handsome with his curling horns. The lambs were very hardy and so appealing. Each grandchild "owned" a ewe, and their lambs when sold gave them a sum of money for their savings accounts.

Jack had always worked hard with his ewes, especially when bad weather meant a lot of yard work with ewes and lambs in individual pens for feeding, or to keep an eye on them for their first few days. It was rewarding to see ewes with a good pair of lambs, but some got called rude names by Jack when they produced one miserable little lamb or two good ones, only to find the ewe had a "deaf tit" as a useless teat was called.

There was much trouble if a mother rejected a lamb for some reason. Perhaps there had been a real mix-up during the night when one enthusiastic ewe would go pushing in to claim another's baby. A rejected lamb would sometimes be put in an empty barrel with its beloved brother and left there for an hour or two, hoping that when brought out to feed, both would be welcome. Sometimes it worked, sometimes it didn't.

The old dodge of skinning a dead lamb and putting the skin on another to give to a ewe with milk but no lamb, was frequently practised with good results. The smelly "jacket" could be discarded after a few days. The sheepdog was sometimes brought in to help by being tied up nearby, thus encouraging the mothering instinct.

There were times when the shepherd's temper ran out, and once I was passing the stable where a temporary pen had been made for a ewe with a dozy lamb, difficult to suckle. Little Mark, then about four, was standing by when I heard Jack say with great feeling, "You blooming, rotten stinking lamb, I could wring your bloody neck!" Mark, in a shocked voice, expressed his feelings with, "Poor lamb, Poppa!"

106

Jack was "Poppa" from the minute Sally came out with her version of "Grandfather" and it has stuck for ever.

The evenings of shepherding held pleasant memories, though driving ewes and young lambs to pastures new was a rather tedious job, needing much patience and good lungs too, when running off to round up strays intent on going in the wrong direction. Our lovely wold landscape spread around us, with high fields and views down the dale or across the plain to York or to Bishop Wilton, or in fields overlooking Worsendale. On fine spring evenings, the lambs gambolled in clutches playing "Follow my leader", or using the muck heap or bales put out for shelter to have a game of "King of the Castle". The ewes eagerly busied themselves at the troughs set out in rows as their supper was carefully trickled out of the sack Jack had been carrying over his shoulder.

On wet, windy nights, this job was not much fun, and shepherding a chore to get finished as quickly as possible. The lambs huddled with humped backs near the straw bales and we, clad in anoraks with hoods up, turned away from the wind. That, I think, sums up most aspects of farming. One is either quietly rejoicing that "God is in His heaven, and all is right with the world" or moaning that "If this goes on, we'll be ruined". The same applies to farm incomes which are not regular as in many businesses, but dependent not only on supply and demand, but the vagaries of our climate and whatever diseases might descend on crops or farm stock.

The suckler herd grew in numbers and eventually replaced all sheep. They lived in the dale or in Wilton grass during the summer but came into the yard for the worst of the winter months. So, going to see the calves was now an evening walk, after leaving the Landrover in a suitable place at the dale end. My dog was not welcome, as cows with calves often object to dogs running around.

The calves came in several colours, some black like their mothers, but gradually with the colour marking of a better bull, the pretty fawns, creams and donkey hues appeared. In winter, when calving took place, they looked grand in the foldyard, which was divided up with gates separating various stages of growing beef.

Pricewise, I see that in 1976 three bullocks cost £153 each.

107

CHAPTER 26

I feel the dogs have been left out of this book so far, and I must remedy the matter as they have all, in their way, been important in our lives. Strangely, perhaps, they are things Jack and I don't share. It has always been a case of "my dog", or "your dog", often without using any name.

Sheepdogs have always been Jack's property and woe betide anyone who interfered. He believed in obedience to one person, himself, which I am sure is right for a working dog.

In the late 'sixties, however, he bought himself an Alsatian pup and considered he was her boss. Dinah her name, short for Dynamite, but a bitch more gentle would have been difficult to find. We all shared in loving her. While following Jack round the farm, never to the sheep, she often accumulated a great deal of mud and I wished he would think of cleaning her down before bringing her into the house. I used to draw attention to the streaky, muddy line along furniture and walls where Di's plumey tail brushed them as she rushed through the house after her master. Her paw marks, too, were very large.

She was not usually a thieving dog, but one day near Christmas Jack called me from the kitchen to open the front door as he was carrying the tree inside. I ran through the hall, quick to obey orders, leaving the Christmas cake which I was about to ice on the side table in front of the window. I wasn't away many minutes, but when I returned, I couldn't believe my eyes. No sign of the cake. After looking around, I spied the remains, which looked like a soggy ball, under the big table, and a very guilty looking Alsatian slunk from her hiding place.

It was an awful waste, but as least I was spared the icing job which I always found very difficult and messy. I had made two cakes as it happened, one with a nut and cherry topping, so that year the little Father Christmas and his gnomes stood on that instead of on bumpy white icing.

We had a succession of small terriers, beginning with Snuff, a tiny Cairn pup, dark brindle in colour which Jack bought when Rachel was just walking on her own. He had always liked the idea of a dog in

108

the house, but Mother wouldn't allow one. I didn't fancy a puppy while the babies were at the floor stage, but here was a toddler and I wasn't pregnant so he came back from Bridlington one day with this wee morsel in his big hands, and a bag of baby food under his arm, as well as a list of instructions on how to look after her. In spite of rejecting the baby food, she grew into a grand little dog.

We all loved Snuff. She trotted miles each day when Jack was tractor driving. After a year or two we thought it would be nice to have pups, so back she went to her breeder's stud dog to be mated. We were very ignorant about dog breeding and were completely taken by surprise when Snuff, after a hard day's tractoring, disappeared one evening and hid herself in the carrycot of dolls under the nursery sideboard. The carrycot was one I had made from an old box and covered with parachute material, the strong yellow kind, and the sideboard was the type with a gap between two cupboards.

We thought it strange that the little dog should want to burrow herself into this squash of dolls and teddies, but we didn't disturb her. Later I went to look and was staggered to find a horrid looking damp, wet white object being licked. I called to Jack and he looked. We both thought this queer looking thing was lifeless, and by the colour must be a premature pup she had aborted. Jack picked up the firetongs to remove the thing from the cot, and it moved so we hastily made more room for it near Snuff, who was glad to continue with her interrupted cleaning process. We could then see that there was fine hair in creamy white. We learned later that "wheaten" Cairns are a throwback to the West Highlands in back breeding. Later that evening two little dark pups arrived. We removed the dolls and put layers of newspapers in this strange maternity bed, and mother and pups stayed there for a few weeks.

We kept the little wheaten dog for Jennifer, but he was run over by a van reversing in the yard when only a few weeks old. It wasn't an easy thing to tell a child running in from school, but later in Snuff's next litter there was another white one and Bengy became part of the family. Both Mother and son moved with us to Cot Nab and lived to a good age.

Snuff was inclined to go broody with false pregnancies, and would make her nest on the landing with a specially chosen woolly animal which she treated just like a pup, gradually leaving it for longer periods till she thought it could be weaned.

Bengy is remembered as the game little terrier with the appalling

109

habit of weeing on the sitting room curtains. He was never caught in the act of lifting a leg, but there was no doubt as to who was responsible for those stains at the right level. Sadly, it was almost impossible to disguise the marks and they were visible till Pam had the curtains bleached and redyed.

Rachel's neurotic Springer Spaniel, the one who tore the kitchen curtains, sadly met his death on the road at an early age. Chunky, another dark shaggy Cairn, was a great character who got on so well with Dinah, but had to be put down before old age after developing a tumour.

After that I had Muffet, a Lakeland cross — some might have said a cross-Lakeland. I loved her dearly, she was a most affectionate little dog, but Dinah hated her, though most of the time she kept this dislike under control. But, with no warning, Muffet perhaps said something very rude, and Dinah would attack Muffet by grabbing her in her strong jaws and refuse to put her down. The first time this happened I was alone on the farm in the garden and I was horrified. Having grabbed Di's collar, I couldn't make her drop Muffet till I grabbed a brick lying near my feet and hit Di's jaws till she opened them. Feeling like a jelly, I comforted my little dog and applied sulphanomide to her wound.

For months there was no more trouble, then little Lucy came screaming to the door one day, "Di's eating Muffet," and off we went again. This time Jack was within call and managed, by twisting Di's collar very tight, to force her to open her mouth. Another gash, which healed, but when a later attack left Muffet badly mauled, we got the vet to put her out of her misery. It was all too traumatic, but no one thought of parting with Dinah!

Later, when the Alsatian was introduced to my dear little West Highland puppy, Kiltie, she was always sweet and gentle with her. It seems dogs can have personality clashes too. The sight of the big Alsatian lying peacefully on the hearthrug with the little pup between her legs made up for all the muddy tail marks, and those large dirty paws. Di lived to a good age, and when she died Tony dug a grave for her in the wood.

CHAPTER 27

Nineteen-seventy-seven was Jubilee Year and, like all other parishes, we got busy with plans to celebrate this occasion. A pie and pea supper was held in the vicarage to raise funds.

The vicar asked for volunteers to ring the church bells, as the Queen had requested. This was to be done throughout the land to mark the great event, and I offered to try my hand. Our bells are not for true campanologists, as there are only three, operated by one person using both hands, and with one foot in the 'stirrup', a large rope which ended in a loop. It is really just a question of co-ordination.

I found, at first, that I needed to concentrate. If anyone spoke to me I went completely wrong and the trouble with bell ringing is that it is heard throughout the village. I was able to ring for ten minutes, taking my place in the relay on Jubilee Sunday, and after that I have kept up this little job whenever needed. It is a good thing for keeping warm in winter and it amuses strangers to the church to see the little old lady performing this strange ritual at the back of the church.

Other Jubilee celebrations included a giant bonfire on the site of the old Wilton Beacon in one of our fields along the Givendale road. The Countess of Halifax put a light to the fire and a vast crowd gave a cheer as flames shot up to the darkening sky. Hot snacks were provided and fireworks added to the jollity. I liked to think of the Queen setting off this chain of fires which took light from each other, as in days of old. I strained my eyes, but couldn't be certain I saw other fires in the distance. The old beacons, which were important signals, would blaze from an iron bucket on top of a tall standard, thus showing up more.

On Jubilee afternoon we had a village tea party with free food for all, fancy dress competitions and sports in the old fashioned way. There was another big celebration at Garrowby, when six hundred folk connected with the estate had dinner in a marquee and a wonderfully exciting firework display further up the park, with set pieces of the Royal family.

We were involved in the Jubilee Drive for the Disabled, and took Tom and Jerry out on three occasions to carry the flag. The idea was to raise money by a series of drives throughout the country, from Windsor to Balmoral, where the flags would be handed to the Queen with a cheque for Riding for the Disabled. The first drive was from Windsor, but routes from all areas continued throughout the summer, ending at Balmoral in the autumn. We joined in the drives from Burton Constable in Holderness, and Castle Howard. Our most local one started in Bishop Wilton with about six turnouts. We left the village and had stops at Bolton Hall, Fangfoss and Stamford Bridge where collecting boxes were rattled. We ended that drive by being welcomed at Aldby Park by Mr. and Mrs. Winn who always offered hospitality to the Driving Clubs, and made us welcome.

We received an invitation to take part in the final drive to Balmoral, but declined as being too far, and too expensive to get there. I had imagined having a tea party in the castle, but heard later that the rally was in the grounds with an inspection by the Queen and Duke in a carriage. Unlike the Yorkshire events, there was no hospitality!

Maureen, when living in the cottage, liked to help with Tom and Jerry and let herself in for quite a lot of harness cleaning. Her eldest daughter, Lucy, had a pony by then, and enjoyed riding. Our girls

Jubilee drive halts at Bolton Hall. Photo by courtesy of Yorkshire Evening Press.

112

kept up their love of riding after they married and had the occasional day's hunting when possible.

Jennifer kept a horse and pony for her girls. Rachel and Norman both hunted when farm work permitted. Norman kept a point-to-point horse and had some success in that line. Rachel went off occasionally to local horse trials and was good at bringing on a young horse to a high standard. Jack and I seldom rode after getting Tom and Jerry, but joined in one or two family rides. Jennifer organised some Pony Club day rides in the Thixendale area and these were a great success and fun for all. The grandchildren joined in, sometimes taking turns with a pony if not enough to go round, and were on a leading rein if not too safe.

We followed in the Landrover as support party with packed lunches aboard and bundles of extra clothing, halters and ponyless children. Rachel joined us and helped Jennifer to control the mob, some of whom wanted to go on at a faster pace. Actually they were all well-mannered ponies and riders and the countryside with grass tracks and dales was ideal. The halfway picnic took place where the two dales widen to make a large flat arena. We helped by holding horses and ponies and handing round drinks. The weather was kind and I am sure that the children will have happy memories, making it all worth the trouble.

I know, too, that the children of our more townee friends who frequently stayed with us for a few days in school holidays look back on the farm visits as high spots in their childhood. I feel that giving children happy memories is an important part of life, though not necessarily over-indulging them with material possessions.

Sponsored walks seemed popular in the 'seventies, and I became involved in this activity too. The first I tried was a seventeen mile walk round Pocklington via Huggate and Millington with John and Rachel Stringer. I remember being very tired on the last stretch of road back into the town, and was expecting better refreshments en route than those offered at Huggate. Perhaps it is as well I have forgotten the cause, and who organised it, but I raised 93p per mile which seems an odd sum.

I enjoyed the walks for both the scenery and the comradeship, and the testing of my capabilities. The Lyke Wake Walk was a very outstanding event. The Cancer Relief Committee, of which we were members, organised the walk and we went off beforehand in the Landrover to reconnoitre a section of the route. It gradually became a big family occasion with Tony, Pam, Maureen and myself walking. Jack and Rachel were acting as a support team with the Landrover while Jennifer volunteered to stay at Cot Nab with all the children. Ken, who worked for us at that time, and a few friends from the village, also joined our little group and Jan Odey went along with us to the starting point at Osmotherley. It semed strange to be setting off at bedtime. We found a huge gathering of would-be walkers on the edge of the village where we had often walked with Tom and Vera years before.

Experienced leaders were in charge of each group, and we were later told that ours was a chap who liked to take the first part at a good pace! I intended to do the first ten miles and was well sponsored for that. I had only done two training walks of about six miles, so by the time we all reached the top of the first stiff climb, I was gasping for breath. I enjoyed the feeling of being part of this great fund raising effort, and when I could breathe easily again, was delighted by the lights of the Cleveland district far below.

The first checkpoint found me glad of a brief rest and a cup of soup, but feeling fit, so I decided to carry on. I shall never forget the next section over the moors, and following the route of the old railway line, when Rosedale was noted for its iron. Although the night was rather dark, the time passed quickly, inspite of aching legs. Jan Odey very kindly slowed her pace to match mine, and we walked together while discussing a great range of subjects. This kept us mentally alert and took our minds off our bodily discomfort.

I was quite thrilled to have done twenty miles, but I wasn't so sure my sponsors would feel the same way, and was ready to collapse in the Landrover to have a drink and a snooze. Jan went steadily on, but I think she had to give up before the finish.

Jack, Rachel and I joined in the cooked breakfast on Wheeldale Moor where Mrs. Goodhart and helpers strove valiantly with picnic stoves in a howling gale. Some of our walkers were looking weary by then, yet the really fit types pressed on to the finish in fine form. Pam had knee trouble, so joined us later and Tony, who made the mistake of wearing new boots, also gave up. Maureen was in real trouble at the last halt near the Whitby road and so also was Gordon from our village. Rachel helped him to change socks and to powder his poor feet. She had also walked the next section with Maureen to encourage her to keep going and, I think, to be near if she collapsed!

Feeling refreshed by my long rest, I opted to be in on the last few miles to Ravenscar so plodded along, feeling so sorry for both Maureen and Gordon who could hardly put one foot in front of the other. I ended up carrying his stick and sweater to relieve him of such burdens. Gordon admitted he had been cocksure about completing the walk and was heavily sponsored so couldn't face the village folk if he gave up. Ken kept going without too much obvious difficulty, but was glad to lie down at the finish and later nearly fainted. This sort of spirit in carrying on really proves that mind can conquer matter, though the 'matter' was in poor shape in many cases.

Most of our group had finished hours ahead. It was mid-morning when the stragglers from Bishop Wilton hobbled over the finishing line, glad to lie down on the roadside. After recovering, and having drinks in the cafe, we piled into the Landrover for the journey home. Tony needed to go to the toilets, but was so seized up that he had to be driven to the door.

When we pulled up in Cot Nab drive, Jennifer came out to greet us with her clutch of children. She was absolutely horrified and very worried to see the state of the crippled walkers. "You must be mad", she said with great feeling, as they hobbled slowly into the house. However she soon got over her shock and quickly provided a good breakfast, though it was lunchtime by then, which was much enjoyed. After that Rachel went home and we thankfully retired to bed.

Later that day Jack and I went to an evening party at Towthorpe where there was a family gathering. As always we enjoyed the company, but I had difficulty in keeping awake. I wasn't too stiff in limbs, and even Maureen made a valiant recovery, walking quite normally within a day or two. The walk raised over £2000 for Cancer Relief, and Maureen was thrilled to have qualified for a Lyke Wake badge.

Another year we made a family contribution on a less arduous sponsored walk, again for Cancer Relief, along part of the Wolds Way. This time three grandchildren did the first ten miles, and we had a happy picnic in Thixendale village. I am not a good walker, but it is surprising how far one can get by gently plodding on. My friend Hilda, also getting on in years, was my companion on much of the Wolds Way walk as the younger ones soon left us, and by the time we reached the long stretch of dale between Fridaythorpe and Millington, I felt as if my boots were two sizes too small, especially when going downhill, but with no hope of giving up until we reached a road once more. Jack was again a support party, and both Hilda and I were glad to get our forms signed for completing twenty miles.

We are fortunate in having good walking country all around us, but it is only when such 'official' walks are organised that we make the effort to spend a whole day in this way. Life still seems ruled by so many 'must do's' each day which can't be ignored. Still, it is better than suffering from boredom.

CHAPTER 28

In the early spring of 1978 poor Lill died peacefully after a gradual deterioration in health. Mother-in-law had also suffered a slow decline both mentally and physically, and had spent her last years at the home of her daughter, Dorothy, being cared for with love and patience with the help of Ted and members of the Clark family.

Both women had been great characters, capable of hard physical work till well on in life's span, and we are grateful to have been close to them. We still frequently recall their activities and quote remarks which have become part of family history.

Other than short visits to friends around this country, we had had very few proper holidays during our married life. Involvement in the horse world took the place of other gadding about, so when Jack was persuaded by our friends Jim and Mary to accompany them on a three week tour of Europe, everyone, including me, who needed little persuading, was astounded. So, early one May morning, after having Jim and Mary with us overnight, we waved goodbye to Maureen and the children and drove down the motorways to Ramsgate. Here we had the excitement and novelty of boarding the hovercraft, but the crossing itself can only be described as boring. In the words of the late Stanley Holloway, "No wrecks, and nobody drowning. In fact, nothing to laff at, at all!" All we could see was grey, misty water, but the smart stewardesses livened the crossing for Jim and Jack.

Jim offered to do all the driving in Europe so we were back seat passengers with Mary as a well-researched navigator. We had two nights in France, finding two very different hotels for overnight stops. In fact, this later afternoon occupation of finding likely looking accommodation was part of the fun of this trip. Jim was the best of the four at making himself understood in French and German, and we enjoyed little walks in town or village in the evening, after some difficulties with dinner menus.

Mid-day meals were always picnic fashion, whatever the weather, but we usually sat out in our folding chairs, buying fresh produce, but also relying on a store of provisions from the car boot. We went round Rheims cathedral and also enjoyed little markets with strange things for sale like live hens and other unusual, to us, produce.

We were fascinated by the strange looking clusters with which some trees were adorned and discovered they were mistletoe. The countryside became really beautiful as we crossed the Jura mountains and descended into Switzerland. Here we spent three days as guests of Adrienne and Peter Jackson. Adrienne was an old convent friend, and co-author of a play we wrote at the age of twelve and which, to our delight, was performed at a school concert. The Jacksons had had very distinguished careers and had lived in Delhi for many years. We had lots to talk about and conversation, as well as the local wine, flowed freely.

I shall never forget arriving at the delightful house under the mountains and looking across Lake Geneva to the Alps beyond, all snow-capped in brilliant sunshine. To one side of the house was a track leading down from the hills above and, with much jingling of bells, came cows on their way to be milked. At that moment, I really felt I was at last in Switzerland as I had imagined it from books and pictures.

I must add, however, that we were all truly thankful for that sunny afternoon as for the rest of our visit the magic of the Alps was shrouded in mist and constant rain. We had a fascinating tour of Chateau Chillon, but in spite of willing the clouds to part while sitting in the boat, we saw only grey countryside. I loved the peacefulness of a church service in a picture-book building set in woodland, though I couldn't follow any of the liturgy, in spite of having attended a French convent!

Sadly, we left the Jacksons to drive over the Jaun Pass which was strikingly beautiful as we sat on a mountainside to eat our picnic and absorb the majestic and peaceful scenery. We had a short stop in Interlaken, where Jack was interested and somewhat appalled by the condition of the landau horses. All the time during our long days of driving, Jack, when not having a snooze, was farming. Cows, sheep and goats were commented on, and while we enthused about the flower-strewn meadows, he could only mutter about spraying being beneficial.

Jack was also interested in the herds of Limousin and Simmental cattle, and the little trailers with milk churns behind, being pulled by someone riding a bicycle or, on one occasion, a moped. All these things fascinated this farmer from Yorkshire, also the cabless tractors with seats for a passenger and the cowsheds attached to the

118

houses. We went into ecstasy over the picturesque barns and the flower-decked houses, mostly with laundry hanging from the balconies, protected by overhanging eaves.

After leaving Liechtenstein with its fairytale castle, we drove over the Aldberg Pass to find ourselves surrounded by snow. The drive was quite hazardous, so we pressed on, after a hurried picnic, to descend to brighter and warmer weather. We stayed that night in a pretty house with a huge painting of St. Christopher on the gable end. We walked through woodlands and over fields near the delightful village of Motz. Later, in the ski resort area, we had quick tours of Innsbruck and Kitzbuhel.

I especially loved Salsburg, where we found "zimmer frei" near the outskirts of the city. We walked round the fascinating streets in heavy rain, but saw more of the city the next morning in sunshine before heading for the motorway, so far avoided, for the last stage of the journey to Vienna.

Here we had a heart-warming reunion with Eva who had visited Jim and Mary as a "deprived" Viennese child after the sufferings that city endured in the war. She had kept in touch over the years. With Eva as our hostess and guide, we spent a week getting to know the beautiful city, the Vienna woods, the Schonbrunn and the Spanish Riding School. The latter experience was quite wonderful as we watched a display by those exquisite white stallions as they performed their graceful movements, surrounded by the elegance of the school, all sparkling chandeliers, marble columns and the large portrait of the founder. We were lucky to have got our tickets, standing room only, as the building was packed. Later, Jack and I especially enjoyed seeing round the stables and the sight of these famous horses at close quarters.

We were driven through the valley of the Danube, which is never blue, and I enjoyed the climb to the castle of Dunstein with its historic connections with our early English king. As a child, I loved the story of Richard the Lionheart and Blondel.

Eva's home was a one-storey farmhouse over two hundred years old, on the outskirts of the city not far from the Schonbrunn. It had not been used as a working farm for many years, and the area surrounding it was now built up with ugly blocks of flats towering above what had once been a village with fields around. The old cowshed, with hayloft above, still remained and the broad doors, as we should call them, opened from the street into the courtyard and large secluded garden with old trees and an orchard. We felt we were in the country, in spite of being in one of the most imposing and important cities in Europe.

In all our three weeks away, we never spoke to other English people. Eva and her family could speak some English and tried hard, especially Eva, with whom we had many laughs over her comical way of turning our language inside out. We, in turn, tried to speak slowly and clearly, while using the most common words. We found ourselves still talking in this fashion to each other, it became such a habit.

During our drive back to England, we had a wonderful day and night in Bad Tolz, a spa village with heavenly mountainous scenery and a balcony on which to sit and quietly absorb it. Again we found flower-decked meadows where the cattle were inside being hand fed. In a Bavarian Beer Keller we joined a party of ladies who were singing round their table after some special meal. We wondered if they were the local W.I.!

One night we stayed near Lake Constanz, and crossed over the next day on the ferry. Jack surprised the shop assistant by purchasing eight large pencils of the souvenir variety. We found everything so dear and with the eight grandchildren, as well as adult family to shop for, we had to look for prices rather than gifts we might have chosen.

Sadly, the Black Forest part of our drive was shrouded in mist and rain, but I found the old part of Colmar in France most exciting and our hotel in what they called "Little Venice" was very olde-world but comfortable. The next day we were fascinated by the grandeur of the Basillica in Domremy and the simple poverty of the humble dwelling where Joan of Arc was born.

Returning to our native shores we 'phoned Maureen and asked her to prepare a good old English stew for our meal the next day, followed by a plain apple pie. It had all been a wonderful holiday and a great experience for Jack and me. Jim had driven 3,500 miles, our store of picnic food had lasted well, and Jack even had some 'baccy' left.

The four of us were still the best of friends, in spite of living in close proximity, but we were very glad to be home again and Jack especially was thankful to put on his working clothes and to become a Wold farmer once more.

CHAPTER 29

In 1979 we had an extra stormy winter. Even to us, so hardened to wild weather, it was remarkable and stands out in memory above all other snow experiences.

Several years earlier we had had a freak storm which caused ice, inches thick, to form on trees, fences and electric wires. We had an extra long time without electricity as poles literally snapped with the weight of ice on the cables and lay across the fields above the dale with wires in tangled confusion. The Electricity Board workers had a very rough time, working in bitterly cold conditions, and we were very thankful to have power again before stuff in the freezer had wasted. Branches fell from trees, the Huggate road was especially affected, and the wood looked incredible with such thick decorations of crystallised ice everywhere.

However, the snow of the '79 winter was for a much longer period which started in the New Year with the usual difficulties in getting about, visits cancelled and roads blocked. In mid-February a blizzard descended on us and the fine snow swirled around the farm for a day and a half. It was a strange, eerie feeling as I tried to scratch a clear space on the window to look out on the wold white world. One afternoon I was determined to walk as far as the drive gate, in spite of being warned, "The wind is like a knife and will cut you in two." I had to turn back after struggling with the elements for a few yards.

Jack and Tony found life very difficult with all the water pipes in the foldyard frozen up. So much time was spent in thawing out as well as battling against snow and wind to even reach the yard. But, foddering up and bedding down had to be done. Tony, of course, was living at Uncleby, but instead of taking about ten minutes to travel to and fro, he took hours. We wanted him to bring Pam and the children to stay with us, but no, he would keep pitting himself stubbornly against the weather, trying to beat it. One day, he took two-and-a-half hours to reach home on a tractor, trying various roads, digging out, and eventually abandoning the tractor to walk the rest of the way.

Fortunately the telephone never failed us, which was a big help, and we could keep in touch with the rest of the family, and make sure

Tony had arrived home. In the mornings Pam could 'phone to see if he had reached Cot Nab. I felt somewhat entombed in my icy retreat, but after the worst of the storm abated, I ventured forth again with my camera and never had I seen such an Arctic sight as the house shrouded in snow, with hardly a window uncovered. Great drifts had piled up, one as high as the front porch, and miniature mountains appeared against the garden hedge and hid the drive gate from sight. The height of snow drifted up near the barn end and the stackyard gate was incredible, but Tony soon made a passage through with the help of tractor and bucket.

Incidentally, when describing this method to a Pocklington friend in such words, "Oh yes, Tony cleared it with the bucket," she looked up at the height of the piled snow and asked with incredulity written over her face, "Just a bucket?"

There was no traffic at first, of course, and the road was silent with the white mounds of stranded vehicles just visible. According to the television and radio news, all the Wolds villages were cut off. There was no description of conditions, for the simple reason that no-one, camera crews or reporters, had ventured forth to find out.

One afternoon, while the roads were still drifted over, Tony found an easier route over the fields so Pam and the children came up to Cot Nab with him for the day. When they were all well wrapped up for the tractor drive home, Jane began to cry. We reassured her thinking she was nervous about getting stuck. "No," she said, "I'm only frightened in case a policeman sees us!" She knew it was against the law to take children on tractors, but we pointed out that being seen by any official person was impossible. We had the countryside to ourselves, like the tribes of old.

As conditions improved, the snow ploughs got through and the police arrived to check on abandoned cars and lorries on the main road. Eventually the road was open with a narrow track for single traffic between walls of snow.

At that stage of this snowy spell, Alison, aged eight, became ill one evening with peculiar symptoms. Maureen asked us to go through to give our opinions and Jack 'phoned the doctor and took her down to the surgery in Pocklington. She was then admitted to hospital in York for observation and to keep a check on her kidneys. Visiting was quite difficult because of road conditions, but the little girl settled happily and began to recover from the strange virus, the name of which I cannot spell! When Alison could come home, the road had blown in again at the top of Garrowby, as it often did in such conditions, so she was transferred from Landrover to tractor and brought over the fields to be made a fuss of on her return. It was some weeks before she was completely recovered.

Our next trouble was a flood in the dairy, due to frozen pipes in the bathroom above. This was an awful discovery one morning, and after the initial mopping up, Tony brought in a large space heater from the tatie store. This made a great deal of noise and fumes, but at least it hastened the drying process.

Then the cylinder in the kitchen airing cupboard developed a leak, and when the plumber tried to reach us his van got stuck in the snow. When he did at last arrive, we were glad to be fixed up again, though we made use of Maureen's hot water system in the meantime.

These snowy conditions, with some easing off, lasted till March. We had a big fund raising planned in the church and this had to be called off at the last minute when a well-known choir from Newcastle became snowbound en route. On another evening we were helping with a Barn Dance in the village hall and this had to be abandoned when a power cut made it impossible. With all the food prepared, we were able to hold it the following night.

Tony had his worst ever journey to work and took four hours to reach us, after many stops to dig himself out. Jack had constant difficulties in getting to the stock at Manna Green. In fact, I think that was the last winter we had any bullocks down there as that track was especially liable to drift in after any snowfall. Again we had short spells of having no traffic past the house, and the men spent a lot of time clearing paths to and from the buildings. Peter, our only regular 'staff', was often unable to drive from Fridaythorpe, so we were shorthanded too.

I usually like the snow and wonder if it is because I was born in a snowstorm and carried out in it at a few days' old, or so Lill told me, but in winters like '79 I had certainly had enough of it. There is a very peaceful and quiet feeling with snow all around, giving a cosy safe haven feeling to being in the house, protected from the elements, perhaps in a primitive way. I get rather a holiday feeling too, with many jobs just left undone and no-one likely to call. Luckily we were never short of food and fuel, though parts of the house were desperately cold.

The worst part was the worry of the men folk getting around and I was always relieved to see Jack back after struggling to reach Manna

Sledging on Garrowby.

Green. It was fortunate that in the extra bad year the sheep had gone and no-one needed to travel far.

CHAPTER 30

So our years at Cot Nab drew to an end. After some years of searching, we found a house we liked in the village below, and Tony, Pam and family moved into the farmhouse, having rather outgrown their cottage. Also, as Tony was taking over the running of the farm, he needed to be living on the premises.

Looking back and reading diaries, I am quite astounded by how much we fitted into our lives, both in work and play. I don't wish to give the idea of a giddy social whirl, but in the way of constantly having friends and relations calling on us and us on them. People dropped in, being on the main road, and Rachel's involvement in the horse world brought her friends to our door when in the neighbourhood. Sometimes they came with horses, and dogs, when competing in events at Bramham or Everingham, so we were able to return hospitality which had been given to us. It surprised them to see our men folk having apple pie 'looances each morning!

At one time Rachel rode horses for other people so owners came to check on training, and to tuck into my baking results round the kitchen table. On two occasions we had her resident pupils for a short period of instruction.

There were spells of having semi-invalid, elderly relations on fairly long visits, as well as the difficult declining years of Mother and Lill, but we were glad that the two who meant so much to our family, and had given out much to us over a long life time, were able to die peacefully in their own beds with family around them.

Whatever difficulties cropped up, I would try to carry on regardless, as it were, with the routine jobs of baking, washing, cleaning, gardening, jam and marmalade making, come what may, with pony activities, visitors in the house and village commitments. Shopping has never taken up a lot of time, perhaps because I don't drive, so I fitted it in to suit Jack's hurried visits to Pocklington. I loved the occasional day in York with a daughter or a friend and enjoyed buying presents, but I may still go weeks without a long shopping session.

Surrounded by family and grandchildren, there were many birthday parties and other celebrations for the older ones. Christmas festivities changed, with the main meal in our kitchen, though we went round the family's houses for other meals, during the ever-lengthening holiday period, usually taking our elderly house guests with us. The family were all good about helping with them, and they loved the happy gatherings after living alone for most of the year.

Sadly now, Lallie and Dorothy are no longer with us, though they visited till very near the end of their lives. Jack's sister, Dorothy, died all to soon, especially after nursing Mother-in-law for so long. Our dear friends Les, Tom, Leonard and Arthur, leave gaps in our lives and, more recently, we were very sad when Margery and Ellis died in Wiltshire within a few months of each other. Margery and I had written long letters every fortnight for more than forty years. It took some time to stop the habit of thinking, "I must write to Marg about that." Other much loved friends and their families keep in touch and we love to meet up, with lots of news to catch up on when they come to our village home.

The kitchen in our "retirement" house is vastly different from the two ("back" and "front") in which I spent so much time in early married life at Kingsfield, but I have never been very quick to move with the times, and am not very gadget minded. My cooker is very basic, and there is no microwave. I love my little electric hand mixer, but I have never wanted a big Kenwood and I am more inclined to reach for the nearest wooden spoon or old fork. I use a small grinder quite often for such things as breadcrumbs, not liking the bought kind, and coffee beans — only for guests — and the liquidiser is lovely for home made soup which we both enjoy. Making use of leftovers always gives me satisfaction. I especially love a kettle which switches itself off and I wonder how I would manage without tea bags which save all that mess in the sink.

I have never craved for a washing up machine, in fact I find that dealing with the dirty pots is a good time to think. Also, it is the cheapest method. I wouldn't like to be without my electric frying pan, or multi-cooker as it is called, as I use it most days in some way or other. It just suits my way of cooking and I don't like cleaning grill pans.

All housewives have different ideas in the kitchen, thank good-ness, and I don't like to be cluttered up or to look after too many time-saving inventions. I cling to my favourite old pots and pans, some of which have been in use for forty years. A fork I inherited from Lill has prongs which vary in length, sloping from one side to the other. It was her special favourite when beating eggs or creaming butter and sugar. It is only a large dinner fork, but the unique appearance bears out the strength of Lill's wrist when cooking in the old fashioned way.

Since living in the village, our family circle has increased with the arrival of grandson Ian to Norman and Rachel, and great-grandson Christopher to Sally and Michael. Christopher has already been held on Jack's old horse on wheels which now lives in a corner of the downstairs loo, and Ian, aged three, is already a knowledgeable little farmer.

Farming continues to face many changes. There is a larger combine at Cot Nab and big bales of straw and silage. There is no haymaking at all, and a field of golden oil seed rape brightens the landscape while causing a plague of black flies in this garden under the wold, at least I am told that is where these creatures come from. They certainly prefer yellow and white flowers and love to alight on clothes of a similar hue.

The need to keep up with progress with a capital "P" has some-

Irene "on the farm" in 1987, with grandson Mark. Photo by courtesy of Yorkshire Evening Press.

127

times led to over-capitalization which is a constant problem for the majority of farmers today as they struggle on, in spite of government and common market interference.

As I write the last chapter of this little book, farming is going through its most difficult phase since the depression of the 'thirties, the decade in which Jack and I first met, and when I heard of the hard times his family had suffered through the falling prices on the agricultural scene.

Now, as well as the worry of making a living in return for long hours of work, farmers have to face all the criticism of the general public, some of whom seem to fancy the countryside as a playground for city folk, idyllic pastures with pretty lambs gambolling about their mothers, and gentle cattle grazing which no-one must ever eat!

Our eating habits have changed very little over the years and, in many ways, Jack and I could be considered at risk with traditional meals which include meat, pastry, butter, puddings and, sometimes, cream. We are fortunate in having good health, so perhaps keeping busy and active is more important than diet. There is no time for boredom, from which many people of all ages suffer, and for that we are thankful.

While remembering our long years together, there have been shadows as well as sunshine in our family life, and farmwise there have been many ups and downs. But I can truly say it has all been a rewarding experience and now, at last, the mud has almost disappeared!